Y0-BRU-630

GLOBAL PERSPECTIVES for LOCAL ACTION

Using TIMSS to Improve
U.S. Mathematics and Science Education

A joint project of
the Committee on Science Education K–12
and
the Mathematical Sciences Education Board

Continuing to Learn from TIMSS Committee
Center for Science, Mathematics, and Engineering Education
National Research Council

Curriculum Lab
College of Education Health & Human Services
University of Michigan-Dearborn

NATIONAL ACADEMY PRESS
Washington, D.C.

NOTICE: The project that is the subject of this report was approved by the Governing Board of the National Research Council, whose members are drawn from the councils of the National Academy of Sciences, the National Academy of Engineering, and the Institute of Medicine. The members of the committee responsible for the report were chosen for their special competences and with regard for appropriate balance.

The National Research Council (NRC) is the operating arm of the National Academies complex, which includes the National Academy of Sciences, the National Academy of Engineering, and the Institute of Medicine. The National Research Council was organized in 1916 by the National Academy of Sciences to associate the broad community of science and technology with the Academy's purposes of furthering knowledge and providing impartial advice to the federal government. Functioning in accordance with general policies determined by the Academy, the Council has become the principal operating agency of both the National Academy of Sciences and the National Academy of Engineering in providing services to the government, the public, and the scientific and engineering communities. The Council is administered jointly by both Academies and the Institute of Medicine. Dr. Bruce M. Alberts, president of the National Academy of Sciences, and Dr. William Wulf, president of the National Academy of Engineering, also serve as chairman and vice-chairman, respectively, of the National Research Council.

The Center for Science, Mathematics, and Engineering Education was established in 1995 to provide coordination of all the National Research Council's education activities and reform efforts for students at all levels, specifically those in kindergarten through twelfth grade, undergraduate institutions, school-to-work programs, and continuing education. The center reports directly to the Governing Board of the National Research Council.

This study was conducted by the Continuing to Learn from TIMSS Committee through a grant from the U.S. Department of Education (grant number R215U970015) to the National Academy of Sciences/National Research Council.

Any opinions, findings, or recommendations expressed in this report are those of the members of the committee and do not necessarily reflect the views of the U.S. Department of Education.

Copies of this report are available online from the Center for Science, Mathematics, and Engineering Education's Web page at <http://www4.nas.edu/csmee/center.nsf> or at <http://www.nap.edu>.

International Standard Book Number 0-309-06530-5

Additional copies of this report are available from:

National Academy Press
2101 Constitution Ave., N.W.
Washington, D.C. 20055
Call 800-624-6242 or 202-334-3313 (in the Washington metropolitan area).

Copyright 1999 by the National Academy of Sciences. All rights reserved.
Printed in the United States of America.

Recommended citation: National Research Council. 1999. Global Perspectives for Local Action: Using TIMSS to Improve U.S. Mathematics and Science Education. Washington, D.C.: National Academy Press.

CONTINUING TO LEARN FROM TIMSS COMMITTEE

Melvin D. George (*Chair*), University of Missouri, Columbia, MO

John R. Brackett, Lake Shore Public Schools, St. Clair Shores, MI

James Hiebert, University of Delaware, Newark, DE

Mark L. Kaufman, Eisenhower Regional Alliance for Mathematics and Science Education Reform, TERC, Cambridge, MA

William Linder-Scholer, SciMathMN, Roseville, MN

Mary M. Lindquist, Columbus State University, Columbus, GA

Michael E. Martinez, University of California, Irvine, CA

Lynn W. Paine, Michigan State University, East Lansing, MI

Deborah Patonai Phillips, St. Vincent-St. Mary High School, Akron, OH

Senta A. Raizen, National Center for Improving Science Education, Washington, DC

Thomas H. Saterfiel, American College Testing, Inc., Iowa City, IA

Thomasena Woods, Newport News Public Schools, Newport News, VA

Staff

Harold Pratt, Project Director

Alfred Young, Administrative Assistant

Steve Olson, Consultant Writer

Diane S. Mann, Financial Officer

COMMITTEE ON SCIENCE EDUCATION K–12

Jane Butler Kahle (*Chair*), Miami University, Oxford, OH

J. Myron Atkin, Stanford University, Stanford, CA

Caryl Edward Buchwald, Carleton College, Northfield, MN

George Bugliarello, Polytechnic University, Brooklyn, NY

Beatriz Chu Clewell, The Urban Institute, Washington, DC

William E. Dugger, Technology for All Americans, Blacksburg, VA

Norman Hackerman, The Robert A. Welch Foundation, Houston, TX

Leroy Hood, University of Washington, Seattle, WA

William Linder-Scholer, SciMathMN, Roseville, MN

Maria Alicia Lopez Freeman, Center for Teacher Leadership in Language and Status, California Science Project, Monterey Park, CA

John A. Moore, University of California, Riverside, CA

Darlene Norfleet, Flynn Park Elementary School, University City, MO

Carolyn Ray, Urban Systemic Initiative, Cleveland, OH

Cary Sneider, Boston Museum of Science, Boston, MA

Rachel Wood, Delaware State Department of Public Instruction, Dover, DE

Robert Yinger, School of Education, Baylor University, Waco, TX

MATHEMATICAL SCIENCES EDUCATION BOARD

Hyman Bass (*Chair*), Columbia University, New York, NY

Jere Confrey (*Vice-Chair*), University of Texas, Austin, TX

Richard A. Askey, University of Wisconsin, Madison, WI

Sherry Baca, Prescott Unified School District, Prescott, AZ

Deborah Loewenberg Ball, University of Michigan, Ann Arbor, MI

Benjamin Blackhawk, St. Paul Academy and Summit School, St. Paul, MN

Richelle Blair, Lakeland Community College, Kirtland, OH

Patricia Campbell, University of Maryland, College Park, MD

Ingrid Daubechies, Princeton University, Princeton, NJ

Karen Economopoulos, TERC, Cambridge, MA

Susan Eyestone, National Parents Teachers Association (PTA), Minneapolis, MN

Lee Jenkins, Enterprise School District, Redding, CA

Glenda T. Lappan, Michigan State University, East Lansing, MI

Miriam Masullo, T. J. Watson Research Center, IBM Corporation, Yorktown Heights, NY

David Moore, Purdue University, West Lafayette, IN

Mari Muri, Connecticut Department of Education, Hartford, CT

Richard Normington, TQM Services Group, Sacramento, CA

Mark Saul, Bronxville Public Schools, Bronxville, NY

Richard Schoen, Stanford University, Stanford, CA

Edward A. Silver, University of Pittsburgh, Pittsburgh, PA

William Tate, University of Wisconsin, Madison, WI

Jerry Uhl, University of Illinois, Urbana, IL

Susan S. Wood, J. Sargeant Reynolds Community College, Richmond, VA

Reviewers

This report was reviewed in draft form by individuals chosen for their diverse perspectives and technical expertise, in accordance with procedures approved by the National Research Council's Report Review Committee. The purpose of this independent review is to provide candid and critical comments that will assist the institution in making the published report as sound as possible and to ensure that the report meets institutional standards for objectivity, evidence, and responsiveness to the study charge. The review comments and draft manuscript remain confidential to protect the integrity of the deliberative process. We thank the following individuals for their participation in the review of this report:

Shelley K. Ferguson, National Council of
    Teachers of Mathematics
Donald Gentry, PolyMet Mining Corporation
Dorothy M. Gilford, Gilford Associates

Henry Heikkinen, University of Northern Colorado

Carol R. Johnson, Minneapolis Public Schools

Lyle V. Jones, University of North Carolina, Chapel Hill

Leon Lederman, Illinois Mathematics & Science Academy, Illinois Institute of Technology, and Fermi National Accelerator Laboratory

Alfred Manaster, University of California, San Diego

Richard McCray, University of Colorado, Denver

Laurie Peterman, SciMathMN

Francisco Ramirez, Stanford University

Harold Stevenson, University of Michigan

Juliana Texley, Anchor Bay School District

While the individuals listed above provided many constructive comments and suggestions, responsibility for the final content of this report rests solely with the authoring committee and the National Research Council.

Contents

Preface

Many words already have been written about the results of TIMSS, the Third International Mathematics and Science Study. By now, many Americans know that U.S. eighth graders and twelfth graders did not perform very well, compared with students in other developed nations, on the achievement tests that were central to TIMSS. The reasons for this unsatisfactory performance are not nearly as clear as the results themselves.

In one state the legislature unilaterally lengthened the school year, at least in part because it assumed that the relatively unsatisfactory performance of U.S. students is a result of spending less time on academic content than do students in other countries, even though the results of TIMSS demonstrate otherwise. Several commentators and officials have stated that U.S. mathematics and science education suffers from curricula that, particularly in mathematics, attempt to cover too many topics at too superficial a level. Some observers have sought to use information from TIMSS to find fault with teacher preparation or student attitudes. Such inferences of cause and effect do not reflect either the complexity of the problem or the richness of the TIMSS results.

This report has been produced at the request of the U.S. Department of Education by the National Research Council's Center for Science, Mathematics, and Engineering Education (CSMEE). Within CSMEE, the Mathematical Sciences Education Board and the Committee on Science Education K–12 acted together to form the Continuing to Learn from TIMSS Committee. The charge to the committee was to help make the findings of TIMSS relevant and useful to leaders in K–12 mathematics and science education and to promote continued public discussion of the many components of TIMSS. As such, the committee has sought to further the center's mission of providing policy analysis and advice through synthesis and interpretation of research so as to promote standards-based reform in mathematics and science education.

The results of TIMSS have direct implications for the implementation of national and state standards in mathematics and science. The TIMSS data relate to the content knowledge and skills of students, the characteristics of mathematics and science curricula, the instructional practices used by teachers, and an array of support issues, including the professional development of teachers. Standards-based reform requires a careful examination of all these aspects of education rather than attempting to focus on one simple change intended to increase student learning.

Given this overall context, this report has several specific objectives that distinguish it from other volumes written about TIMSS. First, this report takes a comprehensive approach to the information generated by TIMSS. It covers all three of the student groups assessed by TIMSS and all of the components of TIMSS, though it does not attempt to deal with all of the tremendous amount of data generated by TIMSS. It highlights important features of the data and stresses the potential uses of the complete TIMSS material, with a focus on areas the committee judged most closely related to student learning in mathematics and science. The committee recognizes that other studies and research results shed light on how to improve the U.S. educational system, but our assignment was to draw specifically on the findings of TIMSS, and we have not gone beyond that charge.

Second, this report is directed to a broad range of stakeholders. It contains material of interest to teachers, parents, administrators, policymakers, curriculum developers, textbook writers, teacher educators, and faculty in institutions of higher education. These stakeholders have many questions about U.S. education. Teachers ask, "Are we teaching too many topics?" Administrators ask, "Should there be additional assessments of student performance?" Policymakers ask, "Should we raise standards for teacher preparation and enhancement, particularly in the areas of mathematics and science?" Parents ask, "Are my children getting the education they will need to lead successful lives?" This report extracts information from the TIMSS data that can inform the answers to such questions.

Finally, this report attempts to inform rather than prescribe. It does not make recommendations for how to reform U.S. education; nor does it lay out a research agenda that would lead to such recommendations. Rather, it illuminates and broadens the range of possibilities to be considered by decisionmakers, whether in the classroom, the boardroom, or the legislative hall. One of the historical problems of U.S. educational reform has been what might be called the pendulum phenomenon. Educational systems tend to overcorrect for what is seen as a problem and end up with a different situation that may be just as unsatisfactory! This report can help decisionmakers dampen the pendulum swings so that steady progress can be made toward a better education in science and mathematics for all students.

This report is based on the premise that there are no panaceas. U.S. education is a complex of interrelated systems that require comprehensive and imaginative analysis and consideration. The results of TIMSS do not suggest that policymakers should replicate in the United States the educational systems of other countries. However, TIMSS can help educators, policymakers, parents, and the general public analyze U.S. education by looking at what is done in other nations. That way, stakeholders can see a wider variety of options than might otherwise be obvious and can understand what the TIMSS results suggest about those options.

The report can be usefully read as a single document. At the same time, it is designed to be used with an accompanying professional development guide in workshops for groups of education decisionmakers. These workshops are meant to support long-range planning efforts aimed at two objectives. The first is to carry out careful local investigations into what is needed to improve mathematics and science achievement in particular schools. The second is to implement changes in schools based on the results of those investigations and on the science and mathematics standards. By providing information from TIMSS, this report can buttress the locally generated research needed to advance standards-based reform—a goal furthered by a November 1999 convocation at the National Academy of Sciences.

The report contains an executive summary and six subsequent chapters. Chapter 1 is a description of the TIMSS project, the kinds of data collected, and the limitations of the data. Chapter 1 also contains references to a number of basic descriptions of TIMSS as well as to several publications that have discussed the validity of the study's results. Chapter 2 presents an overview and several detailed analyses of student achievement in mathematics and science. Following Chapter 2 are three chapters that present the central findings of this report. Chapter 3 looks at curriculum issues, asking how the substance and organization of what is taught in U.S. classrooms can affect student understanding in mathematics and science. Chapter 4 considers U.S. teaching practices, comparing the methods used in this country with those of other countries. Chapter 5 explores the broader educational and social context, such as the time given to various activities, the support given teachers, and student attitudes. Finally, Chapter 6 consists of a number of frequently asked questions about TIMSS with answers drawn from the information that appeared earlier in the report.

The references in this report are intended to alert readers to previously published documents that corroborate and extend particular findings. In addition, a substantial portion of the analysis in this report comes from the unpublished papers commissioned by the committee. Analyses in this report that do not include references generally are based on new work included in these commissioned papers.

The Executive Summary does not include references. References to the material included in the summary can be found in Chapters 1 through 5.

To make this report as useful as possible to its broad range of intended readers, the information in this report is presented in several different ways. While this organization necessarily involves some repetition of ideas, it enables different audiences to use the report effectively and efficiently. The executive summary concludes with a reader's guide to the report, with suggestions of how the report can best be read.

On behalf of the study committee, I acknowledge with deep appreciation the writers of the commissioned papers that formed the basis of our report—Edward Britton, John Dossey, James Hiebert, Jeremy Kilpatrick, Vilma Mesa, Lynn Paine, and Senta Raizen. In addition, we are grateful to those who led and participated in the focus groups that worked with a preliminary draft of this document and helped to improve it considerably. We especially thank project director Harold Pratt and the other dedicated center staff who helped produce the report; consultant Steve Olson, who provided major assistance in writing the report; and representatives of the U.S. Department of Education who worked closely with us on a complex project with a short timeline. All of us hope that this report and the sequence of publications and activities of which it is part will indeed help education leaders strengthen mathematics and science education for all students.

Melvin D. George, *Chair*
Continuing to Learn from TIMSS Committee

GLOBAL PERSPECTIVES for LOCAL ACTION

Executive Summary

In recent years, U.S. mathematics and science education has become a focus of considerable public concern. Much of that concern has been generated by the results of the Third International Mathematics and Science Study (TIMSS), which in the mid-1990s assessed the performance of students in different countries at levels corresponding to grades 4 and 8 and the final year of secondary school (grade 12) in the United States. U.S. students performed well in certain areas, but their overall performance was at best average. Furthermore, the TIMSS data reveal comparative declines in performance from fourth grade to eighth grade and from eighth grade to the final year of secondary school, and in particular areas the performance of U.S. students was weak at all three levels. As states, districts, and individual schools strive to implement high standards for learning in mathematics and science, the results from TIMSS demonstrate that many U.S. students are not now achieving at a high level on an international basis.

A BRIEF DESCRIPTION OF TIMSS (CHAPTER 1)

TIMSS was the largest and most comprehensive study of mathematics and science education ever conducted. It included assessment of the mathematics and science knowledge and skills of more than half a million students from 15,000 schools around the world, including approximately 33,000 U.S. students from more than 500 schools. Students were tested at three levels: the two grades containing the most 9 year olds (population 1, corresponding to grades three and four in the United States); the two grades containing the most 13 year olds (population 2, corresponding to grades seven and eight in the United States), and the final year of secondary school (population 3, corresponding to U.S. high school seniors). Special efforts were taken to ensure that the samples of students tested in each nation were representative. The result is a detailed portrait of student strengths and weaknesses in specific areas of mathematics and science.

Many people describe TIMSS as though it were a "horserace" where all that matters is where the United States ranked compared with other nations. In fact, TIMSS provided much more than just international assessments of student achievement. It analyzed the curricula used in different countries; surveyed educators and students; performed in-depth case studies of schools and educational systems in the United States, Germany, and Japan; and videotaped mathematics classes in eighth grade in those same three countries. These varied international analyses of mathematics and science education provide much to consider beyond the ability of U.S. students to answer particular scientific and mathematical questions.

Taken together, the data provided by TIMSS call attention to factors associated with student achievement, thus identifying promising areas for future study. They also provide deep insights into different ways of teaching and learning, which opens the door to considering new possibilities for U.S. education.

STUDENT ACHIEVEMENT RESULTS (CHAPTER 2)

To examine the school-related factors that need to be considered to improve teaching and learning in mathematics and science, it is useful to know not only the overall achievement results for U.S. students but also more detailed results, such as the particular areas where students did well or poorly.

In mathematics, U.S. students in the upper grade of population 1 (the fourth grade) had average scores somewhat above the international mean when compared with the upper-grade population 1 students in other countries. In science, the only nation's students in the upper grade of population 1 to score significantly better than U.S. students were those of Korea.

Among U.S. students in the upper grade of population 2, science scores remained above the international mean, but students in a number of other countries performed markedly better on average than did U.S. students. In mathematics, U.S. eighth graders' performance dropped below the international mean, with about half the countries in the international sample achieving average scores that were significantly higher than the overall U.S. score.

U.S. students' worst showing was in population 3. In the assessments of general mathematics and science knowledge, U.S. high school seniors scored near the bottom of participating nations. In the assessments of advanced mathematics and physics given to a subset of students who had studied those topics, no nations had significantly lower mean scores than the United States. The TIMSS results indicate that a considerably smaller percentage of U.S. students meet high performance standards than do students in other countries.

Furthermore, many U.S. students are not achieving even at the level indicated by the average U.S. scores. While the variability of U.S. scores was not markedly greater than in other countries, the existing variability in the U.S. scores was strongly linked to the specific classes a student took (for example, regular mathematics versus algebra in middle school or junior high) and to differences among schools. These findings suggest that many students are not being given the educational opportunities needed to achieve at high levels.

At the fourth- and eighth-grade levels, the results were broken down into subareas in both mathematics and science. In science, fourth- and eighth-grade U.S. students exhibited notable weaknesses in the physical sciences. In mathematics, U.S. students' performance tended to be strongest in areas involving whole number operations, fractions, data representation, and probability. Performance was relatively weaker in measurement, proportionality, and (in the eighth grade) geometry and algebra.

At both the fourth- and the eighth-grade levels, U.S. students performed relatively well on mathematics items calling for straightforward computation. However, U.S. students had much weaker abilities overall, compared to students in other nations, to conceptualize measurement relationships, perform geometric transformations, and engage in other complex mathematical tasks. These kinds of abilities are among the learning goals called for by the U.S. national standards and benchmarks for mathematics education and by many sets of state standards, indicating that many U.S. students are not now achieving the objectives of those standards.

CURRICULAR ISSUES (CHAPTER 3)

TIMSS clearly demonstrated that the curriculum affects student achievement. For example, nations tended to perform better in particular areas of mathematics and science emphasized in their countries.

One broad measure of curricular emphasis in mathematics and science is the amount of time given to these subjects in schools. The results from TIMSS demonstrate, somewhat surprisingly, that the time spent on these subjects is higher in U.S. fourth- and eighth-grade classrooms than it is in many other TIMSS countries. Only at the secondary level do students in other countries appear to experience more mathematics and science instruction on average than do students in the United States.

Even when more time is spent on mathematics and science, however, expectations for student learning in the United States may be lower than elsewhere. In the videotaped eighth-grade mathematics classes in the United States, Germany, and Japan, the content of each lesson was compared to the average grade level across all TIMSS countries in which particular topics received the most attention. By this measure, the mathematics content of U.S. lessons was, on average, at a mid-seventh-grade level, whereas German and Japanese lessons were at the high eighth-grade and beginning ninth-grade levels, respectively.

Attention also has focused on the structure of the curriculum, particularly on measures of curricular focus and coherence. Focus refers to the depth with which topics are treated within and across classes. Several lines of evidence point toward a lack of focus in U.S. mathematics and science instruction. According to the TIMSS curriculum analysis, the number of topics in a broad sample of U.S. textbooks was substantially larger than for textbooks in most other countries, and U.S. textbooks include more review exercises and repeat more topics covered in previous grades. Teachers do not necessarily cover everything included in a textbook, but U.S. teachers reported in questionnaires that they teach many more topics over the course of a year than do teachers in Japan or Germany. This rapid movement from one topic to another suggests that U.S. instruction may be more superficial than in other countries, with students often failing to acquire deeper understanding of any particular topic.

Coherence, in contrast, refers to the connectedness of the mathematics and science ideas and skills presented to students over an extended period of time. In a coherent curriculum, new or more complex ideas and skills build on previous learning and applications are used to reinforce prior learning.

Again, several factors suggest a lack of coherence in U.S. curricula, although the evidence is not conclusive. According to the TIMSS curriculum analysis, U.S. textbooks tend to switch from topic to topic much more frequently than do textbooks used in other countries. The videotapes of eighth-grade mathematics classes showed that teachers in the United States switch topics more times than do teachers in Japan and Germany and make fewer references to other parts of a lesson. Also, interruptions of lessons (for example, by public address announcements or outsiders coming into the classroom) are much more common in the United States than in Germany or Japan. When summaries of videotaped lessons from the United States, Germany, and Japan were analyzed by mathematics teaching experts who did not know the country where each lesson was taped, the group found that about 45 percent of U.S. lessons, 76 percent of German lessons, and 92 percent of Japanese lessons achieve a predefined standard of coherence. Using several measures of quality in addition to coherence, these mathematics teaching experts also judged the content of U.S. lessons to be of lower quality than the content of lessons from Japan and Germany.

U.S. national standards and benchmarks in both science and mathematics cite focus and coherence as critical qualities of curricula in those subjects. Unless a clear set of goals is recognized that can establish connections among topics—goals such as those provided by national, state, and local standards in mathematics and science—it can be difficult to construct coherent mathematical and scientific stories in classes that cover large numbers of topics.

INSTRUCTIONAL PRACTICES (CHAPTER 4)

Science and mathematics teachers around the world face many similar challenges. But teachers—and the educational systems of which they are a part—tend to solve similar problems in different ways. These solutions often reflect deeply held beliefs and assumptions that teachers hold about teaching and learning.

The questionnaires completed by teachers at the population 1 and 2 levels show that the structure of lessons has some common features among countries, as well as some interesting differences. For example, the two most common activities in U.S. mathematics teachers' classrooms at the fourth- and eighth-grade levels are teachers working with the whole class and students working individually with assistance from the teacher. In fourth-grade science, another common practice is for the class to work together as a whole with students responding to each other. According to the questionnaires, more than half of U.S. eighth-grade mathematics students received fewer than 20 minutes of instruction on new material in a typical 50-minute class period.

U.S. mathematics and science teachers use tests and quizzes extensively in the eighth grade, and tests and quizzes played a larger role in teachers' reports to parents in the United States than in most other countries. U.S. fourth- and eighth-grade teachers seem to assign amounts of homework comparable to teachers in other countries (though parents and students in other countries may not think of all studying done outside school hours as homework). The United States is one of just a handful of countries where students were frequently given class time for starting homework assignments.

Beneath the observable activities that occur in mathematics and science classes are the external forces and internal motivations that cause teachers to instruct in particular ways. Among the most powerful of these forces are teachers' beliefs and goals, some of which can be inferred from the videotape studies of eighth-grade mathematics in Japan, Germany, and the United States. The videotapes demonstrate that in German mathematics classes there is a concern for technique, where technique includes both the rationale that underlies the procedures and the precision with which the procedure is executed. A good general description of German mathematics teaching at this level would be "developing advanced procedures."

In Japan the teacher carefully designs and orchestrates the mathematics lesson so that students use procedures recently developed in class to solve problems. An appropriate description of Japanese teaching in mathematics would be "structured problem solving."

In the United States the content is less advanced and requires less mathematical reasoning than in the other two countries. The teacher tends to present definitions of terms and demonstrates procedures for solving specific problems, and students are asked to memorize the definitions and practice the procedures. U.S. mathematics teaching in the eighth grade could be described as "learning terms and practicing procedures."

In the United States, skills tend to be learned by mastering the material incrementally, with high levels of success at each step. Confusion and frustration are signs that the earlier material was not mastered. In the style of teaching dominant in the United States, the teacher's role is to shape the task into pieces that are manageable, providing all the information needed to complete the task and plenty of practice.

In Japan, teachers tend to have students struggle with a problem and then participate in a discussion about how to solve it. Confusion and frustration are seen as a natural part of the process and are useful to prepare the students for the information received during the discussion. The teacher's role is to engage the student, reveal the mathematics of interest, and help the students understand the problem so they can attempt to solve it.

A useful way to view these instructional differences among countries is to see them as unified "scripts" for teaching. These scripts are deeply embedded in the culture of each country and can be resistant to change. However, by appreciating one's individual script and the scripts common in other countries, teachers can use TIMSS to begin to examine the assumptions they hold toward teaching and the ingrained ways in which they approach their responsibilities.

The U.S. national standards in mathematics and science call for an approach to teaching in which students actively explore mathematical and scientific ideas, ask questions, construct explanations, test those explanations, and communicate their findings to others. Achieving this kind of instruction in U.S. mathematics and science classes will require reexamining deep-seated beliefs about teaching and learning.

SCHOOL SUPPORT SYSTEMS (CHAPTER 5)

Just as curriculum and instruction affect student performance, the broader culture of a school matters as well. Particularly important aspects of this broader culture include the preparation and support of teachers; attitudes toward the profession of teaching; the attitudes of teachers, students, and parents toward learning; and the lives of teachers and students, both in and out of school.

Not all of these factors are under the control of teachers, school leaders, and policymakers. Nevertheless, the case studies and questionnaires completed by teachers, administrators, and students in TIMSS point to differences in school cultures that can be changed. The results suggest that school cultures are created by the decisions that policymakers, administrators, and teachers make about how to organize teaching and learning.

The structure of the school day and year is quite different in the three countries in which case studies were conducted—the United States, Germany, and Japan. The German school day is much shorter than in either Japan or the United States, and the Japanese school year is longer than in the other two countries. Despite these differences, teachers in all three countries routinely spend time outside of the formal school day to prepare and grade tests, read and grade student work, plan lessons, meet with students and parents, engage in professional development or reading, keep records, and complete administrative tasks.

One of the most significant distinctions between Japanese and U.S. teachers' days is how much time they have to collaborate with colleagues. Compared with Japanese teachers, U.S. teachers spend more of their assigned time in direct instruction and less in settings that allow for professional development and collaboration. In Japan, teachers' time is structured in ways that foster collaboration. For example, they usually share office space with colleagues, and the blocks of time available for Japanese teachers to prepare for classes are typically longer than in most U.S. schools.

Preservice teacher education and later professional development are also important factors influencing the learning environment of students. In the United States, teacher preparation tends to be relatively extended compared with the international average. It is even longer in Germany, where the typical pattern is four to five years of university preparation followed by two years of paid student teaching. In Japan, in contrast, field experiences for preservice teachers typically last a mere two to four weeks, but the Japanese approach views preservice preparation as only a small beginning in a career marked by mentoring relationships.

In-service development also differs markedly from country to country. Japan in the past decade has mandated an intensive mentoring and training program for all teachers in their first year on the job, reflecting the culture's widespread assumption that elders should guide novices. Japanese teachers also rotate among schools every six years, creating career cycles unlike those common in other countries. Professional development opportunities are varied, ranging from formal training at local resource centers to peer observation and informal study groups.

In the United States, professional development is less formal and coherent. Schools and districts offer a range of staff development programs, but these tend to be short term, vary widely in focus, and often appear to teachers as a menu of unrelated opportunities. Although some districts engage in more systematic efforts at sustained professional development, including sustained mentoring programs, short-term workshops remain the dominant format.

Educational systems vary in the degree to which they treat teachers either as professionals or as skilled workers. These differences in treatment surface in such forms as hiring practices, the organization of teacher time, the degree to which teachers control aspects of their work and time, opportunities for continued learning, and the fostering of collegial relationships among educators.

The material and symbolic benefits accorded teachers reflect the extent to which they are treated as either professionals or skilled workers. For example, teachers in Japan are paid more in comparison to other workers with similar backgrounds than are teachers in the United States. Employment benefits also tend to be better in Japan and Germany. On the other hand, Japanese teachers report that their profession is respected but not as much as it was in the past.

Finally, student attitudes toward mathematics and science, another powerful influence on the culture of mathematics and science education, tend to be positive across countries. Most U.S. fourth and eighth graders report that they like both mathematics and science, although fourth graders are more positive than eighth graders. However, students in some of the highest-performing countries recorded markedly lower perceptions of their own performance compared with students elsewhere, suggesting that students in high-performing countries may work especially hard to meet perceived shortcomings.

The national mathematics and science standards call attention to the critical importance of the broader culture in shaping teaching and learning in the United States. Teachers need the support of administrators, policymakers, parents, and the broader society to make lasting improvements in mathematics and science instruction.

A READER'S GUIDE TO THIS REPORT

The value of TIMSS lies not only in the questions it answers but also in those it raises. Reflection on how education is conducted in different countries is a rich source of insight into the potential of alternative educational approaches. The findings of TIMSS do not suggest that the United States should seek to replicate aspects of other countries' educational systems. However, the findings offer many ways to increase understanding of the U.S. educational system and to identify possible changes that could improve teaching and learning.

To foster careful analysis and creative

thinking about educational practices in the United States, Chapters 3, 4, and 5 of this report include sets of questions keyed to the topics discussed in those chapters. These questions are directed toward a wide range of readers with interests in the education system, including parents, teachers, administrators, policymakers, textbook writers, publishers, those who work in science centers and museums, scientists and engineers, business people, university faculty, and the general public. By examining these questions, readers of the report are invited to consider both the steps that can be taken to improve U.S. education and the additional information needed to help establish future directions.

Different readers might be particularly interested in certain chapters of the report. For example, curriculum developers, parents, and teachers might want to concentrate on Chapter 3, "What Does TIMSS Say About the Mathematics and Science Curriculum?" Teachers investigating alternate classroom strategies might want to focus on Chapter 4, "What Does TIMSS Say About Instructional Practices?" Administrators and teacher educators can read about the culture of U.S. education in Chapter 5, "What Does TIMSS Say About School Support Systems?" The final chapter, "Frequently Asked Questions About TIMSS," summarizes important information from earlier in the report in a question-and-answer format.

CHAPTER ONE

What Is TIMSS ?

Since the early 1960s, education research organizations in the United States and other countries have conducted several major international comparisons of student performance in mathematics and science. For example, the 1981 Second International Mathematics Study (SIMS) measured mathematics achievement among 13 year olds in 14 industrialized and 6 developing nations. It focused on curricula, classroom processes, preparation of teachers, and attitudes of teachers and students toward mathematics (McKnight et al., 1989). Similarly, in 1991 the International Assessment of Educational Progress assessed the mathematics and science skills of samples of 9 and 13 year olds from the United States and 19 other countries. In this and earlier assessments the scores of U.S. students generally fell into the lower part of the distribution of scores for the students sampled (Lapointe et al., 1992; U.S. Department of Education, 1992).

The Third International Mathematics and Science Study (TIMSS), which was conducted over the course of several years in the mid-1990s, was by far the largest and most ambitious international assessment of student performance in mathematics and science. Like previous studies, TIMSS set out to assess how well students in different countries are able to solve mathematical and scientific problems at different stages of their education. In addition, TIMSS sought to set these achievement data in a much richer context than had been available before. It gathered an extensive variety of information about curricula, teaching practices, and the influences on teachers and students both inside and outside the classroom.

The data provided by TIMSS, along with information from previous international comparisons, have been an extremely valuable resource. They have called attention to factors associated with student achievement, thus identifying promising areas for future study. They have provided deep insights into different ways of teaching and learning, which has made possible reexamination of conventional U.S. practices. By opening a window onto the educational systems of other countries, TIMSS has revealed new possibilities for U.S. education.

For example, information from TIMSS and from previous studies has made it possible to answer questions that have immediate implications for teaching and learning. Do U.S. students know as much about mathematics and science as students in other countries? Are U.S. curricula as demanding or as well structured as the curricula in other countries? What do U.S. teachers actually do in the classroom, and how does this compare with what they say they are doing? How much support do teachers receive for mathematics and science education? How much time do students spend working in outside jobs, doing homework, and watching television? All of these questions and many more can be addressed using information gathered by TIMSS.

However, even a data set as extensive as that offered by TIMSS cannot answer many important questions in education. In particular, the educational system is so complex that it is difficult to link cause and effect conclusively. The TIMSS data cannot be used to select one or two education changes, such as revamping the curriculum or increasing the amount of homework students do, that will guarantee higher student performance. Nor was TIMSS designed to be an experimental study, where different students are randomly assigned to carefully balanced groups, the groups are treated differently, and the effects of those differences are then measured.

It also is important to recognize what TIMSS did not set out to study. It did not, for example, gather information about educational financing at the local and class levels. TIMSS also gathered less information about students in their last year of secondary school and their teachers than it did for students in populations 1 and 2. It did not assess the performance of students in college or ask whether U.S. college students eventually catch up with their international peers in areas where they have fallen behind. Finally, TIMSS gathered more information about mathematics than about science in many areas—for example, classes were videotaped only in mathematics, and some questionnaires were distributed only to mathematics teachers and students.

THE POPULATIONS STUDIED

TIMSS focused on students at three stages of their education: midway through elementary school, midway through lower secondary school, and at the end of upper secondary school (U.S. Department of Education, 1997a, p. 6). The selection of students therefore considered both their ages and their grade level.

At the elementary school level, TIMSS assessed the performance of students in the two adjacent grades containing the most 9 year olds (Table 1-1). In the case of the United States, this "population 1" group was drawn from grades three and four. Twenty-six countries participated in this part of the study (Table 1-2). In the United States, achievement data were collected from a sample of 3,819 third graders and 7,296 fourth graders in 189 public and private elementary schools (Martin et al., 1997, p. A-14; Mullis et al., 1997, p. A-16).

At the lower secondary school level, students were studied in the two adjacent grades containing the most 13 year olds. In the United States, this "population 2" group encompassed grades seven and eight. Forty-one countries participated in this part of the study. In the United States, 185 public and private junior high and middle schools participated in the tests, with a sample of 3,886 seventh graders and 7,087 eighth graders being tested (Beaton et al., 1996a, p. A-14; 1996b, p. A-14).

The third population studied consisted of students in their final year of secondary school. Because secondary schools conclude at different ages in different countries, the students in this population were not all the same age. In the United States, the students in this population 3 group were seniors in high school. A sample of about 11,000 high school seniors from 211 public and private high schools participated in the assessment of general knowledge in mathematics and science (Mullis et al., 1998, p. B-19). Twenty other countries also participated fully in this part of TIMSS. In addition, two sets of 16 countries, including in both cases the United States, tested smaller groups of students in physics and advanced mathematics.

Most of the testing occurred two to three

TABLE 1-1 Groups of Students Studied in TIMSS

Population 1	Students in the pair of adjacent grades containing the most 9 year olds	Grades three and four in the United States
Population 2	Students in the pair of adjacent grades containing the most 13 year olds	Grades seven and eight in the United States
Population 3	Students in their final year of secondary school, regardless of age	Grade 12 in the United States

TABLE 1-2 Countries That Participated in the TIMSS Student Performance Assessments

Population 1	Population 2	Population 3 Math. and Sci. Literacy	Population 3 Advanced Mathematics	Population 3 Physics
Australia	Australia	Australia	Australia	Australia
Austria	Austria	Austria	Austria	Austria
—	Belgium (Flemish)	—	—	—
—	Belgium (French)	—	—	—
—	Bulgaria	—	—	—
Canada	Canada	Canada	Canada	Canada
—	Colombia	—	—	—
Cyprus	Cyprus	Cyprus	Cyprus	Cyprus
Czech Republic	Czech Republic	Czech Republic	Czech Republic	Czech Republic
—	Denmark	Denmark	Denmark	Denmark
England	England	—	—	—
—	France	France	France	France
—	Germany	Germany	Germany	Germany
Greece	Greece	—	Greece	Greece
Hong Kong	Hong Kong	—	—	—
Hungary	Hungary	Hungary	—	—
Iceland	Iceland	Iceland	—	—
Iran, Islamic Rep.	Iran, Islamic Rep.	—	—	—
Ireland	Ireland	—	—	—
Israel	Israel	—	—	—
—	—	Italy	Italy	—
Japan	Japan	—	—	—
Korea	Korea	—	—	—
Kuwait	Kuwait	—	—	—
Latvia	Latvia	—	—	Latvia
—	Lithuania	Lithuania	Lithuania	—
Netherlands	Netherlands	Netherlands	—	—
New Zealand	New Zealand	New Zealand	—	—
Norway	Norway	Norway	—	Norway
Portugal	Portugal	—	—	—
—	Romania	—	—	—
—	Russian Fed.	Russian Fed.	Russian Fed.	Russian Fed.
Scotland	Scotland	—	—	—
Singapore	Singapore	—	—	—
—	Slovak Republic	—	—	—
Slovenia	Slovenia	Slovenia	Slovenia	Slovenia
—	South Africa	South Africa	—	—
—	Spain	—	—	—
—	Sweden	Sweden	Sweden	Sweden
—	Switzerland	Switzerland	Switzerland	Switzerland
Thailand	Thailand	—	—	—
United States	United States	United States	United States	United States

Note: Dashes indicate that the country did not participate in that part of the assessment.

Source: U.S. Department of Education, 1996, 1997b, 1998.

months before the end of the 1994-95 school year. In each country, the tests were translated into the primary language or languages of instruction. All testing in the United States was done in English.

Worldwide, more than a half million students from some 15,000 schools participated in the TIMSS achievement tests, including approximately 33,000 U.S. students from more than 500 schools.

RANGE OF DATA

Much of the media coverage of the TIMSS results focused on the achievement comparisons, and the United States' ranking among nations is what many people still remember best about TIMSS. However, the achievement data were just one part of TIMSS.

TIMSS used five different methods to collect data: student achievement tests, questionnaire responses, curriculum analyses, videotapes of classroom instruction, and case studies of policy issues (Table 1-3).

TIMSS Achievement Tests

The half-million students that participated in TIMSS took tests that were an hour and a half long (U.S. Department of Education, 1997a, p. 7). The tests included both multiple-choice problems and free-response exercises that asked students to solve problems in their own words. Each student answered a subset of the total set of questions, allowing for a broader testing of content than if all students answered all questions. A smaller number of students in many countries also completed hands-on performance assessments designed to gauge their skills in particular areas of mathematics and science.

The content to be tested in each subject and at each grade level was determined through a consensus process involving all of the partici-

TABLE 1-3 Areas in Which Data Were Gathered in TIMSS

Data Gathered	Pop. 1 Math.	Pop. 1 Science	Pop. 2 Math.	Pop. 2 Science	Pop. 3 M&S Literacy
Achievement tests	X	X	X	X	X
Teacher questionnaires	X	X	X	X	
Student questionnaires			X	X	
Administrator questionnaires	X	X	X	X	X
Curriculum analyses	X	X	X	X	X
Videotaped lessons			X		

Note: More information was gathered for mathematics than for science, and more information was collected at the population 2 level (seventh and eighth grades in the United States) than at either the population 1 (third and fourth grades) or population 3 (final year of high school) levels. The curriculum analysis covered all grades, not just those sampled in the TIMSS achievement tests. Lessons were videotaped only of mathematics classes and only in three countries: the United States, Germany, and Japan. Case studies were made of selected features of educational systems in those same three countries.

pating countries. An international analysis of curricula was conducted so that the development of the assessments could reflect the curricula of participating countries. Pilot testing of assessments further reduced any bias toward or against particular countries.

To avoid making statistically meaningless distinctions that come with a strict ranking, U.S. publications describing the TIMSS achievement results divide participating countries into three bands: those that performed significantly better than the United States, those that performed at a level indistinguishable from that of the United States, and those that performed significantly worse than the United States. The results of the achievement tests are described in Chapter 2.

Questionnaires

Students, teachers, and administrators at the schools that participated in TIMSS answered questionnaires about important aspects of education. Students answered questions about their mathematics and science classes and about their attitudes toward these subjects. Teachers answered questions about their teaching practices, their backgrounds, and their instructional goals as well as their attitudes toward science and mathematics. School administrators were asked about school policies and practices, curriculum, staffing levels, and the availability of instructional resources, including science laboratories.

Curriculum Analyses

Researchers analyzed more than 1,000 mathematics and science textbooks and official curriculum guides from participating countries to determine what TIMSS researchers termed the "intended curriculum" (Beaton et al., 1996a, p. A-1). For each of these documents the subject-matter content, sequencing of topics, and expectations for student performance were coded. Questionnaires distributed to education experts within each country supplemented the curriculum analyses.

Videotapes of Classes

In the United States, Germany, and Japan, between 50 and 100 eighth-grade mathematics classes in each country were videotaped (Stigler and Hiebert, 1997, pp. 14-21; Stigler et al., 1999, p. 9). The tapes were digitized, transcribed, and translated, giving researchers virtually instant access to any part of the lessons. The tapes then were coded for the occurrence of various events, teaching strategies, and content elements, so that the lessons could be analyzed quantitatively. In addition, teacher questionnaires concerning the specific class sessions videotaped were collected, so that stated intentions and the actual teaching evident in the classroom could be compared.

The students and teachers in most of these tapes were guaranteed confidentiality, and those tapes are seen only by researchers. Several "public use" tapes also were collected in each country as examples to help communicate the results of the study (U.S. Department of Education, 1997c; Stigler et al., 1999, p. 9). Teachers and students who appear in these tapes agreed to have their lessons made available for public viewing.

Case Studies

Also in the United States, Germany, and Japan, teams of bilingual researchers did a number of case studies of educational policies and practices (Stevenson and Nerison-Low, 1997; Stevenson, 1998, pp. 524-529). About 20 researchers, all of whom were familiar with the culture in which they worked, spent two to three months conducting interviews, conversations, and classroom observations in three metropolitan areas in each country. The researchers conducted interviews with pupils, teachers, parents, policymakers, education authorities, and other persons engaged in the education enterprise. A computer network linked all the researchers and enabled them to store and retrieve verbatim transcripts, observational records, and other field notes. The case studies focused on four topics: education standards, teacher education and teachers' working conditions, dealing with differences in student ability, and the place of school in adolescents' lives.

CRITICISMS OF TIMSS

Because international comparisons of student performance inevitably call attention to U.S. educational practices, all such comparisons have received intense scrutiny. TIMSS has been no exception.

Questions and criticisms of TIMSS and other international comparisons have fallen into several broad categories (Bracey, 1996). The first concerns whether comparable groups of students in each country are included in a study. For example, if one country tested only groups of students who would be expected to score higher on a test, its results may be skewed higher compared with results from a country that tested a more representative group of students.

The designers of TIMSS took a number of steps to avoid this selection bias (Beaton et al., 1996a, pp. A-9 through A-19). First, criteria were established to ensure that the schools selected and the students tested achieved certain participation rates. Countries could exclude a small percentage (less than 10 percent) of certain kinds of schools or students who would be very difficult or too resource intensive to test (e.g., schools for students with special needs or schools that were very small or located in extremely remote locations). Most countries excluded a much smaller percentage of schools and students than specified, and countries that did not meet this criterion were noted in the results.

Of the remaining schools, countries had to achieve participation rates of 85 percent of the schools and students selected (or a combined rate of 75 percent) to satisfy the sampling guidelines. Within each school, countries had to use random procedures to select the classes to be tested. All of the students in the selected classes participated in the TIMSS testing. An international committee scrutinized this selection and testing process to ensure that the students who participated in TIMSS were randomly selected to represent all students in their respective nations.

When nations did not meet the established standards, these exceptions were noted in analyses of the results. For instance, of the 26 nations that participated in the population 1 assessment, 17 met or came close to meeting all of the selection standards for the study. The other 9 countries did not meet the standards—for example, because the percentage of schools, teachers, or students declining to participate exceeded the sampling guidelines. These nations and the problems they had meeting the guidelines are identified in the published results.

A related set of criticisms of TIMSS involves the assessments of students at the end of their secondary education. For populations 1 and 2—except for a handful of TIMSS countries—virtually all children are enrolled in school and are therefore eligible to take the test. However, students not still enrolled in school by their final year of secondary school were not tested in TIMSS. Furthermore, because secondary school ends at different points in different countries, the average age of these students varied from country to country, and some have asked whether it is fair to compare students of different ages (Rotberg, 1998). Finally, because testing occurred toward the end of the school year, questions also have arisen about whether the U.S. seniors were motivated to do well on the test.

The average age of the U.S. students tested in population 3—18.1 years—was somewhat less than the average age of all the students in this population who took the test—18.7 years (Forgione, 1998). However, the mathematics and science literacy assessment at the population 3 level sought to measure knowledge that should have been learned several years earlier, lessening the effect of age differentials. Finally, one objective of this part of TIMSS was to assess performance when students in each country are deemed ready to enter the adult world, and differences in age are one measure of

how this determination varies across countries.

Another major criticism of TIMSS and other international achievement tests is that the results depend largely on the sequence of topics within each country's overall curriculum and do not reflect the quality of those curricula or teaching practices. The first half of this point is certainly valid. As shown in Chapter 4, what students are taught does have a direct impact on their performance, and one of the goals of TIMSS was to explore this connection between curriculum and student knowledge.

TIMSS was designed, however, in such a way as to minimize the effects of curriculum differences. Extensive information on curriculum was factored into the tests' design so that they reflected the mathematics and science curriculum of all TIMSS countries and did not overemphasize what is taught in only a few. Questions on the test also were divided into separate subcategories so that performance in specific areas of mathematics and science could be compared with the detailed curriculum in different countries.

A related criticism of TIMSS suggests that widespread access to higher education in the United States reduces the importance of the subpar high school achievement results. But a substantial portion of high school graduates do not attend college—fewer than two-thirds of 1994 U.S. high school graduates were enrolled in a college or university the following fall. Many students who attend college never obtain a degree, and many of those who do take little mathematics or science in college. Furthermore, many students who do go to college need to take remedial courses in mathematics or science—one in four freshmen in 1995 took remedial math.

A final and much broader objection to TIMSS is that the countries compared are so different culturally that comparisons of student performance have little relevance (Bracey, 1997, 1998). For example, according to this line of argument, the extensive academic work that many Asian students do outside school to prepare for high school and college entrance exams makes comparisons with U.S. students meaningless. Critics of international comparisons also point to such intangibles as creativity, motivation, perseverance, flexibility, and entrepreneurial skill as positive outcomes of U.S. education that international comparisons cannot measure.

As with the other differences among countries, cultural differences are part of what TIMSS set out to study (Baker, 1997a, 1997b). TIMSS gathered data on a wide variety of cultural influences, such as the amount of time students spend working, watching television, and doing homework; the background and experiences of teachers; and student and teacher attitudes toward mathematics and science. Each of these factors is a potential explanation for differences in student understanding of mathematics and science, as are differences in curriculum and instruction.

Moreover, differences in culture do not invalidate comparisons of students. TIMSS set out to measure basic skills that people must use throughout their lives such as reasoning, application of knowledge, and designing multistep solutions. Parents, educators, and policymakers are legitimately interested in how these skills vary from country to country.

In general, the TIMSS results are broadly consistent with the findings of earlier and more limited comparisons of international academic performance (Stedman, 1997). Younger students in the United States tend to do better in international comparisons than do older students. In particular areas, U.S. students perform much more poorly than do students in other countries, and this poor performance persists across the various grades tested. For example, at both the fourth and the eighth grades the comparatively weakest part of U.S. students' performance in science was in the physical sciences, a finding that also applies in the last year of high school.

WHAT OTHER STUDIES ARE UNDER WAY?

TIMSS generated a huge body of data. Even today some of the basic studies from TIMSS have not yet been released, and reanalyses of data already released will continue for years to come.

At the same time, new international studies are now being planned that will extend the results from TIMSS. The most directly related follow-up study is known as the TIMSS Repeat Project, or TIMSS-R. This study gathered achievement data very similar to the TIMSS data for the upper grade of population 2 (eighth grade in the United States) in 1999. Because TIMSS tested students in 1994-95, the students in population 1 for the original TIMSS will be in population 2 for TIMSS-R, making it possible to compare the progress of different groups of students over time. TIMSS-R also will include background questionnaires for students, teachers, and schools to investigate instructional practices and aspects of the learning environment. In 1998, 31 countries conducted field tests for the study, and 8 additional countries planned to join the main data collection stage.

As a separately funded project, the U.S. Department of Education is sponsoring a videotape project to extend the TIMSS videotape study of eighth-grade mathematics teaching in the United States, Japan, and Germany. The new videotape study will encompass additional countries as well as an analogous taping and analysis of eighth-grade science teaching.

Another closely related project is the Program for International Student Assessment (PISA) being conducted by the Organization for Economic Cooperation and Development (OECD). PISA will measure students' knowledge, skills, and competencies in three areas— reading, mathematics, and science. The overall strategy is to collect in-depth information on student outcomes in one of these three domains every three years, with a minor focus on the other two content domains. The major focus for the first survey, which will take place in the year 2000, is on reading, with a minor focus on mathematics and science. The major focus in 2003 will be mathematics, and in 2006 it will be science. The subjects of this study will be nationally representative samples of 15 year olds, the highest age at which school enrollment in OECD countries is essentially universal. About 25 OECD countries are expected to participate, and they likely will be joined by a number of other countries.

These studies and the continuing analysis of results from TIMSS will provide a continual flow of new information about mathematics and science education in the United States and in countries around the world. The challenge, which is taken up in the next four chapters of this report, is to use this information to help guide improvements in the curricula, teaching, and educational environments experienced by all students.

CHAPTER TWO

What Does TIMSS Say About Student Achievement?

TIMSS provided a wealth of information on the knowledge and skills of students in mathematics and science. In each of the three student groups studied by TIMSS, the achievement tests included questions on different topics in mathematics and science, so that particular strengths and weaknesses could be measured. In addition, for populations 1 and 2, TIMSS tested students in adjacent grades, providing a measure of gains achieved between those two grades (third and fourth grades and seventh and eighth grades in the United States).

As described in the previous chapter, the achievement test results were just one of many kinds of data produced by TIMSS. Taken together, these data provide an unprecedented amount of information about the teaching practices, educational policies, school characteristics, student attitudes, and other factors that contribute to academic strengths and weaknesses in each participating country. However, as might be expected, the achievement scores have garnered the most public attention. Much of this attention has focused on the "horserace" aspects of TIMSS—how did U.S. students do compared with students in other countries? This emphasis on the bottom line of the achievement scores can obscure potentially more interesting results. For instance, in what subjects did U.S. students perform well and in which did they perform poorly, and how are these areas aligned with common U.S. mathematics and science curricula? Do U.S. students learn as much from grade to grade as students in other countries? How are student scores linked to the characteristics of the schools they attend?

The questions in the TIMSS achievement tests were based on the curricula in participating countries, and to the extent that these curricula reflected national standards in science and mathematics, the tests provide a general indication of how well students are meeting those standards. However, the TIMSS achievement tests were not aligned with the standards of any one country, such as those of the United States (Beaty, 1997, pp. 27-28; National Research Council, 1997, p. 3). The TIMSS results therefore do not provide a direct measure of whether students are achieving the standards and benchmarks specified by national organizations (National Council of Teachers of Mathematics, 1989; American Association for the Advancement of Science, 1993; National Research Council, 1996) or the standards in place at the state, national, or local levels.

Nevertheless, an important message from the achievement results is that there is considerable room for improvement in U.S. education (Table 2-1). While U.S. fourth graders scored considerably above the international average in both science and mathematics, U.S. eighth graders scored just above the average in science and below it in mathematics. U.S. high school seniors performed even less well overall in tests of general mathematical and scientific knowledge and had particularly low mean scores on the assessments of advanced mathematics and physics. On an international scale, U.S. students, particularly in the upper grades tested, are not achieving high standards.

Furthermore, many students are not achieving even at the level indicated by the average U.S. score. While the variability of U.S. scores was not markedly greater than in other countries (Stedman, 1997), variability among student scores in the United States was strongly linked to the specific classes a student took (for example, regular mathematics versus algebra in middle school or junior high) and to differences among schools (Schmidt et al., 1999, pp. 163-180). These findings suggest that many students are not being given the educational opportunities needed to achieve at high levels.

This chapter looks first at the achievement results in mathematics and then at those in science. It applies a somewhat different analysis to each discipline, partly to reveal particularly noteworthy results and partly to demonstrate different ways of using the achievement results. Much more extensive analyses of the achievement results, along with sample problems, can be found in the reports from the TIMSS International Study Center (Beaton et al., 1996a, 1996b; Harmon et al., 1997; Martin et al., 1997; Mullis et al., 1997, 1998) and in the summary reports from the U.S. Department of

Education (1996, 1997b, 1998). The publicly released test items for populations 1, 2, and 3 also can be ordered from the TIMSS International Study Center or can be downloaded from the World Wide Web at http:/www.csteep.bd.edu/TIMSS1/TIMSSPublications.html#International.

MATHEMATICS ACHIEVEMENT

In mathematics the population 1 assessment asked students 102 questions overall. Each student tested answered just a subset of questions, but by combining student responses it is possible to calculate "student scores" for the entire set of achievement items. Using this method, U.S. fourth graders answered 64 of the 102 questions correctly on average, which is 10 to 13 items below the average performance of students in the top four countries and in a band of performance comparable with that found in the Czech Republic, Iceland, and Canada (Table 2-2a). In the population 2 assessment, U.S. eighth graders answered a mean of 80 questions out of 151 correctly (Table 2-2b). Students in the four top-scoring countries—Singapore, Japan, Korea, and Hong Kong—answered an average of between 105 and 119 questions correctly.

The questions on the population 1 assessment were grouped into six areas:

- whole numbers
- data representation, analysis, and probability
- geometry
- patterns, relations, and functions
- fractions and proportionality
- measurement, estimation, and number sense

U.S. students at grade four achieved above the international mean performance in the first four of the content areas listed above. (This analysis considers just the students in the upper grades of both populations 1 and 2.) They did less well in the area of fractions and proportionality (though still near the international mean) and less well than that in the area of measurement, estimation, and number sense.

The population 2 assessment was divided into six somewhat different topic areas:

- data representation, analysis, and probability
- fractions and number sense
- geometry
- algebra
- measurement
- proportionality

Only in the first two areas listed above—data representation, analysis, and probability, and fractions and number sense—did U.S. eighth graders score near the international mean. They scored below the international mean in geometry, algebra, measurement, and proportionality.

In the final year of secondary school the performance of U.S. students is even farther below international standards (U.S. Department of Education, 1998, pp. 17-18). The population 3 results can be difficult to evaluate because of sampling issues and other problems mentioned in Chapter 1. For example, of the 21 countries that participated in the general

TABLE 2 1 Overview of Student Achievement Results from TIMSS

Population 1 Upper-Grade Science		Population 1 Upper-Grade Mathematics		Population 2 Upper-Grade Science		Population 2 Upper-Grade Mathematics	
Nations	Avg.	Nations	Avg.	Nations	Avg.	Nations	Avg.
Nations with Average Scores Significantly Higher than the U.S.		**Nations with Average Scores Significantly Higher than the U.S.**		**Nations with Average Scores Significantly Higher than the U.S.**		**Nations with Average Scores Significantly Higher than the U.S.**	
Korea	597	Singapore	625	Singapore	607	Singapore	643
		Korea	611	Czech Republic	574	Korea	607
Nations with Average Scores not Significantly Different from the U.S.		Japan	597	Japan	571	Japan	605
		Hong Kong	587	Korea	565	Hong Kong	588
		(Netherlands)	577	(Bulgaria)	565	Belgium-Flemish▲	565
Japan	574	Czech Republic	567	(Netherlands)	560	Czech Republic	564
United States	565	(Austria)	559	(Slovenia)	560	Slovak Republic	547
(Austria)	565			(Austria)	558	Switzerland▲	545
(Australia)	562	**Nations with Average Scores not Significantly Different from the U.S.**		Hungary	554	(Netherlands)	541
(Netherlands)	557					(Slovenia)	541
Czech Republic	557			**Nations with Average Scores not Significantly Different from the U.S.**		(Bulgaria)	540
		(Slovenia)	552			(Austria)	539
Nations with Average Scores Significantly Lower than the U.S.		Ireland	550			France	538
		(Hungary)	548	England*▲	552	Hungary	537
		(Australia)	546	Belgium-Flemish▲	550	Russian Federation	535
		United States	545	(Australia)	545	(Australia)	530
England▲	551	Canada	532	Slovak Republic	544	Ireland	527
Canada	549	(Israel)	531	Russian Federation	538	Canada	527
Singapore	547			Ireland	538	(Belgium-French)	526
(Slovenia)	546	**Nations with Average Scores Significantly Lower than the U.S.**		Sweden	535	Sweden■	519
Ireland	539			United States ▲	534		
Scotland ▲	536			(Germany)*▲	531	**Nations with Average Scores not Significantly Different from the U.S.**	
Hong Kong	533	(Latvia (LSS))	525	Canada	531		
(Hungary)	532	Scotland▲	520	Norway	527		
New Zealand	531	England*▲	513	New Zealand	525	(Thailand)	522
Norway	530	Cyprus	502	(Thailand)	525	(Israel)*	522
(Latvia (LSS))	512	Norway	502	(Israel)*	524	(Germany)*	522
(Israel)	505	New Zealand	499	Hong Kong	522	New Zealand	508
Iceland	505	Greece	492	Switzerland▲	522	England*▲	506
Greece	497	(Thailand)	490	(Scotland)●	517	Norway	503
Portugal	480	Portugal	475			(Denmark)	502
Cyprus	475	Iceland	474	**Nations with Average Scores Significantly Lower than the U.S.**		United States▲	500
(Thailand)	473	Iran, Islamic Rep.	429			(Scotland)	498
Iran, Islamic Rep.	416	(Kuwait)	400			Latvia (LSS)▲	493
(Kuwait)	401			Spain●	517	Spain	487
				France	498	Iceland	487
International Avg. = 524◆		International Avg. = 529◆		(Greece)	497	(Greece)	484
				(Iceland)	494	(Romania)	482
				(Romania)	486		

TABLE 2-1 Continued

Population 1 Upper-Grade Science		Population 1 Upper-Grade Mathematics		Population 2 Upper-Grade Science		Population 2 Upper-Grade Mathematics	
Nations	Avg.	Nations	Avg.	Nations	Avg.	Nations	Avg.
				Nations with Average Scores Significantly Lower than the U.S.		**Nations with Average Scores Significantly Lower than the U.S.**	
				Latvia (LSS)▲	485	Lithuania*	477
				Portugal	480	Cyprus	474
				(Denmark)	478	Portugal	454
				Lithuania*	476	Iran, Islamic Rep.	428
				(Belgium-French)	471	(Kuwait)	392
				Iran, Islamic Rep.	470	(Colombia)	385
				Cyprus	463	(South Africa)	354
				(Kuwait)	430		
				(Colombia)	411	International Avg. = 513★	
				(South Africa)	326		
				International Avg.=516★			

Population 3 Science Literacy		Population 3 Mathematics Literacy		Population 3 Advanced Mathematics		Population 3 Physics	
Nations	Avg.	Nations	Avg.	Nations	Avg.	Nations	Avg.
Nations with Average Scores Significantly Higher than the U.S.		**Nations with Average Scores Significantly Higher than the U.S.**		**Nations with Average Scores Significantly Higher than the U.S.**		**Nations with Average Scores Significantly Higher than the U.S.**	
Sweden	559	(Netherlands)	560	France	557	Norway	581
(Netherlands)	558	Sweden	552	(Russian Fed.)	542	Sweden	573
(Iceland)	549	(Denmark)	547	Switzerland	533	(Russian Fed.)	545
(Norway)	544	Switzerland	540	(Australia)	525	(Denmark)	534
(Canada)	532	(Iceland)	534	(Denmark)	522	(Slovenia)	523
New Zealand	529	(Norway)	528	(Cyprus)	518	(Germany)	522
(Australia)	527	(France)	523	(Lithuania)	516	(Australia)	518
Switzerland	523	New Zealand	522	Greece	513	(Cyprus)	494
(Austria)	520	(Australia)	522	Sweden	512	(Latvia)	488
(Slovenia)	517	(Canada)	519	Canada	509	Switzerland	488
(Denmark)	509	(Austria)	518	(Slovenia)	475	Greece	486
		(Slovenia)	512			(Canada)	485

TABLE 2-1 Continued

Population 3 Science Literacy		Population 3 Mathematics Literacy		Population 3 Advanced Mathematics		Population 3 Physics	
Nations	Avg.	Nations	Avg.	Nations	Avg.	Nations	Avg.
Nations with Average Scores not Significantly Different from the U.S.		(Germany)	495	**Nations with Average Scores not Significantly Different from the U.S.**		France	466
		Hungary	483			Czech Republic	451
		Nations with Average Scores not Significantly Different from the U.S.				**Nations with Average Scores not Significantly Different from the U.S.**	
(Germany)	497			(Italy)	474		
(France)	487			Czech Republic	469		
Czech Republic	487			(Germany	465		
(Russian Fed.)	481	(Italy)	476	(United States)	442	(Austria)	435
(United States)	480	(Russian Fed.)	471	(Austria)	436	(United States)	423
(Italy)	475	(Lithuania)	469				
Hungary	471	Czech Republic	466	**Nations with Average Scores Significantly Lower than the U.S.**		**Nations with Average Scores Significantly Lower than the U.S.**	
(Lithuania)	461	(United States)	461				
Nations with Average Scores Significantly Lower than the U.S.		**Nations with Average Scores Significantly Lower than the U.S.**		NONE		NONE	
				International Avg. = 501		International Avg. = 501	
(Cyprus)	448	(Cyprus)	446				
(South Africa)	349	(South Africa)	356				
International Avg. =500		International Avg. = 500					

Notes:

1. In the United States the upper grade of population 1 corresponds to grade 4, and the upper grade of population 2 corresponds to grade 8.

2. Nations not meeting international guidelines are shown in parenthesis.

3. Nations in which more than 10 percent of the population was excluded from testing are shown with an *. Latvia is designated LSS because only Latvian-speaking schools were tested, which represents less than 65 percent of the population.

4. Nations in which a participation rate of 75 percent of the schools and students combined was achieved only after replacements for refusals were substituted are shown with a ▲.

   ◆ The international average is the average of the national averages of the 26 nations.

   ★ The international average is the average of the national average of the 41 nations.

   ● The country average for Scotland (or Spain) may appear to be out of place; however, statistically, its placement is correct.

   ■ The country average for Sweden may appear to be out of place; however, statistically, its placement is correct.

Source: Business Coalition for Education Reform, 1998, pp. 6-7.

TABLE 2-2a Mean Number of Questions Answered Correctly by Upper-Grade Students in Population 1 for Countries Participating in Both the Population 1 and Population 2 TIMSS Assessments

Country	Mean Number of Items Correct for Population 1 Upper-Grade Students (102 items total)
Singapore	77.52
Korea	77.52
Japan	75.48
Hong Kong	74.46
Czech Republic	67.32
United States	64.26
Iceland	64.26
Canada	61.20
England	58.14
Cyprus	55.08
New Zealand	54.06
Norway	54.06
Portugal	48.96
Iran	38.76

Source: John Dossey, 1998, "Some Implications of the TIMSS Results for Mathematics Education," paper commissioned by the Continuing to Learn from TIMSS Committee.

TABLE 2-2b Mean Number of Questions Answered Correctly by the Upper-Grade Students in Population 2 for Countries Participating in Both the Population 1 and Population 2 TIMSS Assessments

Country	Mean Number of Items Correct for Population 2 Upper-Grade Students (151 items total)
Singapore	119.29
Japan	110.23
Korea	108.72
Hong Kong	105.70
Czech Republic	99.66
Canada	89.09
New Zealand	81.54
Norway	81.54
United States	**80.03**
England	80.03
Iceland	75.50
Cyprus	72.48
Portugal	64.93
Iran	57.38

Source: John Dossey, 1998, "Some Implications of the TIMSS Results for Mathematics Education," paper commissioned by the Continuing to Learn from TIMSS Committee.

mathematics and science literacy assessment, only 8 met the TIMSS guidelines for sample participation, and the United States was not among those 8 (Mullis et al., 1998, p. 3). Nevertheless, if potential difficulties with the data are kept in mind, the test scores still reveal much about the mathematical abilities of U.S. high school seniors. On the assessment of general knowledge in mathematics—the level of mathematics deemed necessary to function effectively in society as adults—14 countries outperformed the United States, 4 countries were not significantly different, and 2 countries were below. On the assessment of advanced mathematics—which was given to students who had taken or were taking precalculus, calculus, or Advanced Placement calculus in the United States—11 countries outperformed the United States and no countries performed worse.

The data reveal that U.S. eighth graders performed at a lower level compared with other countries than did U.S. fourth graders, and relative performance declined again between the eighth and twelfth grades. For example, student performance in the area of measurement, which was already below average at grade four, was the lowest recorded area of U.S. performance across the two populations in grade eight. In the areas of geometry and data representation, analysis, and probability, student performance started above the international mean in grade four and moved to below it in grade eight. Mathematical literacy was not broken into subareas at the population 3 level.

Despite the often-expressed concern that the basics are slighted in U.S. education, U.S. students did not falter on items calling for straightforward algorithmic work relative to their international peers. For example, U.S. fourth graders performed at or above the international mean on the following questions:

- selecting the largest of 2735, 2537, 2573, and 2753
- selecting the answer to 6000 - 2369
- selecting what part of a figure was shaded
- finding the solution to a word problem involving decimal subtraction

At the same time, fourth graders were below the international mean in solving a number problem for a missing addend and using a ratio to calculate a larger proportional value, which are both considered more advanced skills in the United States.

At the grade eight level, U.S. students performed at or above the international mean in:

- selecting the answer to 6000 - 2369
- writing a fraction larger than 2/7
- writing a weight that might have rounded to a given number
- selecting the correct ratio of red to total paint in a mixture

However, eighth graders fell below the mean in determining the portion of a purchase that belonged to one individual and in determining the number of one part of a proportion given the ratio of parts and the total.

Overall, student performance in grade eight in the areas of number and operation-based computations was at or above the international level. In other mathematical content areas, however, U.S. performance was much weaker. At the grade eight level, several of the items indicated that U.S. students have a weak ability to conceptualize measurement relationships. For example, when asked which of four students had the longest pace given a table of paces it took each student to measure a room's width, only 48 percent of U.S. students selected the student who used the fewest paces, versus the international average of 74 percent.

Geometry performance showed perhaps the greatest relative change between grades four and eight. At grade four, U.S. student performance was over one-half of a standard deviation above the international mean for the countries that participated in both the population 1 and population 2 assessments. By grade eight, it had decreased to almost one standard deviation beneath the mean for this set of countries. At grade four, U.S. performance showed that students were near or above the mean in locating objects on a grid and in dealing with visual perception and line reflections. These items were in large part items dependent on following simple directions and knowing the names of figures.

By grade eight, U.S. students had fallen behind in identifying a rotated figure, identifying necessary properties of a parallelogram, and selecting congruent triangles based on angle measurement and figure reflection properties. However, they remained at the international average in determining which of five given points fell on a line determined by two other points when the points were given as ordered pairs. At the eighth-grade level, the differences seemed to fall along the lines of being able to use definitions and properties to reason about geometric figures and actions in the plane. At grade four the emphasis in the TIMSS assessments was on name recognition, where U.S. students did relatively well. At grade eight, the emphasis was on understanding the properties of mathematical objects and the consequences of actions on those objects, where more U.S. students faltered.

A related observation about the skills conveyed in mathematics classes came from the TIMSS videotape study (Stigler and Hiebert, 1997; Stigler et al., 1999). Researchers used the tapes of eighth-grade mathematics classes to compare the kinds of mathematical reasoning evident in the lessons. Using a reasonably generous definition of deductive reasoning, in which conclusions are drawn from axioms or premises through explicit logical steps, no examples of such reasoning were found in the U.S. lessons. In contrast, there were instances of deductive reasoning in 53 percent of Japanese lessons and 10 percent of German lessons. This feature of U.S. lessons seems to point toward an emphasis on fact and definition and a lack of emphasis on deductive reasoning.

The national standards in mathematics and many sets of state standards call for students to achieve proficiency in exploring mathematical ideas, conjecturing, using logical reasoning, and solving nonroutine problems. The relative weaknesses of U.S. students in areas of the TIMSS assessments related to these abilities indicates that many students are not yet achieving the standards' objectives.

SCIENCE ACHIEVEMENT

As in mathematics, the scores of U.S. students in science were relatively high on an international scale at the population 1 level and declined at the population 2 and 3 levels. U.S. third and fourth graders scored among the highest of students in all TIMSS countries. At the population 2 level, U.S. students ranked with those in a band of countries close to the international mean. During the final year of secondary school, a much greater number of nations scored significantly higher than did the United States. According to TIMSS, U.S. students are leaving high school with substantially less proficiency in science than are students in many other countries.

The calculated gains in student learning between adjacent grades also point to declining achievement compared to other countries. As explained in the previous chapter, TIMSS sampled from the two adjacent grades with the most 9 year olds for population 1 and with the most 13 year olds for population 2. Therefore, it is possible to look at how much students "gained" in learning between grades three and four and between grades seven and eight, even though the students tested actually were in successive grades rather than being the same set of students tested in two successive years.

For population 1 the United States ranked eleventh in achievement gain between grades three and four out of the 17 countries following all of the sampling procedures (Martin et al., 1997, p. 29). This relatively modest gain from grade to grade compared to other countries foreshadows the relative decline in the U.S. standing between populations 1 and 2. For population 2, U.S. students ranked 26th in gain between grades seven and eight out of the 27 countries following all of the sampling procedures (Beaton et al., 1996b, p. 29).

As with the mathematics scores, the science scores were broken down into a number of subject areas and subareas. For population 1 the four main content areas were:

- earth science
- life science
- environmental issues and the nature of science
- physical science

One notable aspect of performance in these four areas involves the early appearance of weaknesses in the physical sciences among U.S. students (Schmidt et al., 1999, p. 120). Even in population 1, where only Korean students scored significantly better than U.S. students overall in science, the deficit of learning in the physical sciences among U.S. students is apparent. U.S. population 1 students did not score significantly above average in any of the four subareas within the physical sciences, whereas Korean and Japanese students scored significantly higher in all four and Dutch students in three of the four.

Another measure of the relative weakness of U.S. students in the physical sciences involves the 12 performance tasks given at both the population 1 and population 2 levels (Harmon et al., 1997). All but one of the five science tasks dealt with physical science topics, and U.S. students scored at or below the international average on all of these. For example, U.S. students did particularly poorly with a task

involving batteries at the eighth-grade level, where they scored 11 percentage points below the international average and 20 percentage points (or more) behind Singapore, England, Romania, and Switzerland, the highest-scoring countries.

At the population 2 level, the performance tests were broken down into five broad categories:

- earth science
- life science
- environmental issues and the nature of science
- chemistry
- physics

Again, eighth-grade students in the United States notably lagged in their performance in physics. Population 2 students scored near the bottom of the distribution of 22 countries in four of the six subareas within the physical sciences (Schmidt et al., 1999, pp. 125-127).

At the population 3 level, the measured level of overall U.S. science performance was very low. Even countries that explicitly track their students into different streams in upper secondary school—for example, academic, technical, vocational, and general—demonstrated higher student achievement for mathematics and science literacy in the latter three streams than the United States does for its academic students (Mullis et al., 1998, p. 83). And for the physics test, which measured the proficiency in physics of students who were completing or had completed a physics or advanced physics course, U.S. student achievement was the lowest of the 16 countries participating. Even comparing the best U.S. students—the 1 percent of U.S. seniors taking Advanced Placement physics courses—versus all of the students taking the advanced physics test in other countries (representing 10 to 15 percent of all students in their final year of secondary school), U.S. students could do no better than low average (U.S. Department of Education, 1998, p. 52).

These results clearly demonstrate that in the United States a considerably smaller percentage of students meet high performance standards in science than do students in other countries. And even the small percentage of "elite" U.S. students do not excel compared to the larger proportion of "elites" in other countries.

One notable aspect of the U.S. science performance at all three levels is the relative lack of gender differences. Even at the population 3 level, which is the only level with a statistically significant difference between genders, this difference is the lowest (along with that of Cyprus) among the 21 participating countries (Mullis et al., 1998, p. 52). Historically in the United States, gender differences favoring males in science achievement have been considerably greater than is the case for the TIMSS results. Perhaps the results reflect the considerable attention given to involving and supporting female students in the sciences. Indeed, TIMSS data for the United States show equal numbers of male and female students taking science in the twelfth grade, although the specific courses taken are not indicated (Mullis et al., 1998, p. 90).

CONCLUSION

The 1998 draft revision of the mathematics standards issued by the National Council of Teachers of Mathematics reaffirms the NCTM's commitment "to providing the highest-quality mathematics instructional program for all students." Similarly, the *National Science Education Standards* issued by the National Research Council (1996) describe standards as "criteria to judge progress toward a national vision of learning and teaching science in a system that promotes excellence."

By these measures the results of TIMSS suggest that U.S. students are falling short. Although U.S. fourth graders compare favorably to their international peers, U.S. eighth graders and high school seniors achieve at a lower level than do students in many other countries.

The next three chapters of this report examine factors related to student learning in mathematics and science. Chapter 3 looks at selected qualities of science and mathematics curricula. Chapter 4 discusses instructional practices, including examples of representative classrooms in different countries. Chapter 5 considers the support systems available to teachers and students in seeking to achieve high standards.

What Does TIMSS Say About the Mathematics and Science Curriculum?

CHAPTER THREE

Many factors determine what a student learns in school, but TIMSS clearly demonstrated that one important factor is the curriculum to which students are exposed. For example, each nation performed more and less well in particular areas of mathematics and science emphasized in that country. U.S. 13 year olds scored second among TIMSS countries in the area of "life cycle and genetics"—topics that tend to be highlighted in middle school and junior high school curricula. But they scored near the bottom of TIMSS countries in the area of "physical changes," reflecting the lower emphasis in U.S. curricula on the physical sciences (Schmidt and McKnight, 1998; Schmidt et al., 1999, p. 124).

The TIMSS framework defines "curriculum" very broadly. TIMSS considered the "intended" curriculum set forth in guidelines and by texts, the "implemented" curriculum actually delivered by a teacher, and the "achieved" curriculum measured by the results of assessments (Beaton et al., 1996a, p. A-1). This chapter takes a more restricted view of curriculum, focusing largely on the content that is taught and the organization of that content.

The content specified by a curriculum forms one of many sets of expectations that affect student learning. These expectations come from many different sources. Official documents such as curriculum guides and standardized tests specify knowledge and skills for students to master. Teachers expect certain levels of student performance and use formal and informal assessments to determine if those levels have been achieved. Parents, peers, and the broader culture exert important influences on student behaviors.

Educational standards at the national, state, and local levels also establish sets of expectations for student learning in mathematics and science. National standards and benchmarks in mathematics and science (National Council of Teachers of Mathematics, 1989, 1998; American Association for the Advancement of Science, 1993; National Research Council, 1996) outline in broad terms what students should know, understand, and be able to do in each subject. State and local standards vary widely in specificity, format, and links to assessments, but they, too, create frameworks of expectations for students to meet.

Most standards documents emphasize the need for *all* students to achieve high levels of mathematics and science literacy, yet different groups of students often are subject to different sets of expectations. Sometimes these expectations are set deliberately, as when a student takes an advanced placement course or undergoes some form of educational tracking. Other differentiated expectations may be more subtle or even inadvertent but can still have a major influence on students. For example, community norms might be different for boys than for girls, or low-performing students might be put in classes or student groupings where only low-level skills are expected.

In considering how a curriculum in mathematics or science is related to student learning, it is critically important to think explicitly about the expectations embodied in that curriculum. To what extent are expectations embodied in instructional materials, in course requirements, or in tests and grades? How are expectations conveyed to students, and do those messages conflict with others that students receive inside or outside school? Are students provided with the means necessary to achieve the demands made of them?

This chapter begins by examining how much time students spend studying mathematics and science, the subjects introduced at different grade levels, and the curricular tracks into which students are divided. The remainder of the chapter investigates the structure of mathematics and science curricula along two related dimensions: focus and coherence.

At the beginning of each of the major sections of this and the following two chapters are questions like the ones in the accompanying box. These questions suggest ways for teachers, administrators, policymakers, parents, textbook writers, curriculum developers, and others to examine local aspects of schooling in light of the results from TIMSS.

QUESTIONS RELATED TO CURRICULAR EXPECTATIONS

• How do current classroom expectations for student achievement compare to national, state, and local standards in mathematics and science?

• What expectations concerning mathematics and science education are held by parents, business leaders, and community leaders? How do these relate to expectations within schools?

• Are there different expectations for different groups of students? If so, are these based on background, ability, or other factors such as socioeconomic variables? Are these expectations educationally beneficial or harmful for the members of these different groups?

• How are the academic expectations embodied in the curriculum communicated to students? How do these messages affect student motivation, course taking, and achievement?

• How is it determined whether expectations for mathematics and science learning are being met by students?

• How can expectations be increased? What is the anticipated outcome of increased expectations?

TIME AND TRACKING

Perhaps the most general characteristic of mathematics and science curricula is the amount of time given to these subjects in schools. Despite a widespread belief that students in other countries spend more time studying mathematics and science than do U.S. students, the results from TIMSS indicate otherwise—at least in elementary school and early secondary school. According to the questionnaires distributed as part of TIMSS, time spent on mathematics and science instruction is higher for populations 1 and 2 in U.S. classrooms than in many other TIMSS countries (U.S. Department of Education, 1996, p. 39; 1997b, p. 40). U.S. fourth graders, for example, spend more time in class each week studying mathematics and science than do their average international counterparts (Figure 3-1). U.S. eighth graders spend more hours per year in mathematics classes than do students in Japan and Germany (Figure 3-2), even though the U.S. school year is only about 180 days,

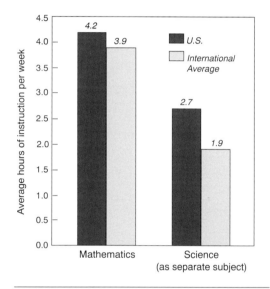

FIGURE 3-1 Reports from the upper grade of population 1 teachers on the average number of hours of mathematics and science instruction per week. Source: U.S. Department of Education, 1997b, p. 40.

compared with 188 days in Germany and 220 in Japan.

The amount of time devoted to mathematics and science in populations 1 and 2 varies somewhat from student to student in the

QUESTIONS RELATED TO TIME AND TRACKING

- What mathematics and science courses are required for all students at what grade levels?
- How much time do the fourth- and eighth-grade curricula give to mathematics and science, both per week and per year? How do these amounts compare with international averages?
- How much mathematics and science do students take specifically in high school? Are these amounts sufficient for them to achieve literacy in these subjects?
- How are the mathematics and science curricula in different grades related to each other, both within and across subjects? Do the structure and content of these classes enable students to have smoothly articulated learning experiences in mathematics and science?
- Does tracking result in different students being exposed to substantially different curricula? How would this differential exposure to mathematics and science be expected to affect their learning of these subjects?

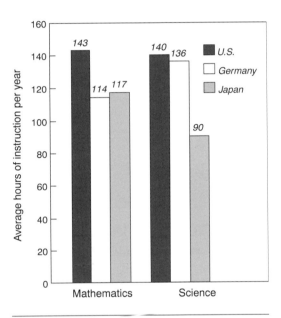

FIGURE 3-2 Number of hours of mathematics and science instruction per year for eighth graders. Source: U.S. Department of Education, 1996, p. 39.

United States, partly because of tracking designed to address differing abilities (Schmidt et al., 1999, pp. 57-59). However, the greater impact of tracking appears to be on the content and skills to which different groups of school children are exposed, not on the total amount of time spent on the subjects (Schmidt et al., 1999, p. 24).

In the final year of secondary school, exposure to mathematics and science among U.S. students is more variable. While 66 percent of graduating students in the United States were currently taking mathematics, the average in all the countries participating in the general assessment of mathematics and science knowledge was 79 percent. In science, 53 percent of U.S. students were taking a science course, compared with 67 percent for all TIMSS countries. In fact, the United States is unique in the high percentage of students taking either no or only one science course (93 percent) in their final year of secondary school (Mullis et al., 1998, p. 89). It should be noted, however, that Norway, which has an even greater percentage of students taking no science course in their final year, scored well above the international average in the population 3 science literacy test.

Among the TIMSS countries, mathematics curricula tend to be more similar than science curricula. Most countries roughly agree on the progression of topics to introduce at different grades, even when they do not place the topics

TABLE 3-1 Mathematics Topics Intended for Introduction at Various Grades

Grade Group	Topics that Half the Countries Intended for Introduction in Grade Group	
1 through 3	Whole number: meaning Whole number: operations Whole number: properties of operations Common fractions Estimating quantity and size	Measurements: units Measurement: perimeter, area, and volume 2-D geometry: basics 2-D geometry: polygons and circles Data representations and analysis
4 through 6	Decimal fractions Relationships of common and decimal fractions Percentages Properties of common and decimal fractions Negative numbers, integers and their properties Number theory Rounding and significant figures	2-D geometry: coordinate geometry 3-D geometry Geometry: transformations Constructions using straightedge and compass Proportionality concepts Proportionality problems Equations and formulas
7 and 8	Rational numbers and their properties Real numbers, their subsets, and their properties Exponents, roots, and radicals Exponents and orders of magnitude	Measurement: estimation and errors Geometry: congruence and similarity Proportionality: slope and trigonometry Patterns, relations, and functions
9 through 12	Complex numbers and their properties Counting (permutations and combinations) Vectors Uncertainty and probability	Infinite processes Change Validation and justification Structuring and abstracting

Source: Schmidt et al., 1997a, p. 66.

in exactly the same grade or treat them the same way (Table 3-1). In addition, almost all countries introduce many more mathematics topics in the earlier grades than in later grades (Schmidt et al., 1997a, p. 66).

In U.S. high schools, certain topics in mathematics traditionally have been reserved for specific grades. Though integrated mathematics courses have become more common, in many schools algebra often is still reserved for grades 9 and 11 and geometry for grade 10. In contrast, a common pattern in European countries and Japan is to combine algebra and geometry in a single class and to introduce them at an earlier age.

Curricular approaches to science are more varied than for mathematics. For example, many countries teach little or no formal science until grade three or later (Schmidt et al., 1997b, pp. 82-86). These include Argentina, Belgium (Flemish and French), Bulgaria, China, the Czech Republic, Hungary, Japan, the Netherlands, the Philippines, Romania, Singapore, and Spain.

Beginning in lower secondary school, about 60 percent of the countries require that students take more than one science course simultaneously (Schmidt et al., 1997b, pp. 36-38). For example, in the Russian Federation, students have separate courses in biology and earth science in lower secondary school, to which are added courses in physics and chemistry in upper secondary school.

The average numbers of topics introduced in science remain roughly comparable across grade levels (Table 3-2). However, the U.S. science curriculum contrasts with that of many other countries by eliminating rather than adding topics in each grade of upper secondary school (Schmidt et al., 1997b, pp. 82-85). In fact, the majority of countries intend that more topics be covered per year in the upper-secondary grades than does the United States. This probably results from the "layer cake" approach to the U.S. science curriculum, where students focus on just a single disciplinary area each year.

Countries also vary with respect to the different curriculum streams through which science courses are offered (Schmidt et al., 1997b, p. 32). There is only one stream in Japan (though there is tracking with respect to the rigor of the curriculum in upper secondary school). In the Netherlands, in contrast, there are four streams (some of which are considered harder than others), though all four require combined physics and chemistry, biology, and geography and earth science in grades 9 through 11.

The order of the topics introduced in science and mathematics does not reveal the depth or rigor with which those subjects are taught. However, many U.S. mathematics and science classes appear to cover topics at a more elementary level than is the case in other countries. For example, in the videotapes made of 231 eighth-grade classes in the United States, Germany, and Japan, the content of each lesson

was compared to the average grade level across all TIMSS countries in which particular topics received the most attention. By this measure, the mathematics content of U.S. lessons was, on average, at a mid-seventh-grade level, whereas German and Japanese lessons were at the high eighth-grade and beginning ninth-grade levels, respectively (Stigler et al., 1999, p. 43-44). At least in eighth-grade mathematics—and quite likely in science and at other grade levels as well—U.S. instruction is not at the world-class level established as a goal by national, state, and local standards in mathematics and science.

One interesting aspect of the TIMSS data is that they do not reveal any obvious advantages to having a nationally set curriculum—at least not in mathematics, where the data from TIMSS are more plentiful. For example, when countries are sorted by whether control over the curriculum is focused on national, regional, or local authorities, no obvious performance patterns emerge in mathematics. Countries with centralized curricula appear at both the top and bottom of the list. The results of TIMSS therefore do not indicate whether adopting a national curriculum will or will not improve student achievement.

FOCUS AND COHERENCE

The TIMSS data have been used to support a wide variety of observations about U.S. mathematics and science curricula—for example, that these curricula are "a mile wide and an inch deep" or that mathematics and science curricula suffer from a "splintered vision." A particularly useful way to assess the validity of these observations is to analyze the

TABLE 3-2 Science Topics Intended for Introduction at Different Grade Levels

Grade Group	Topics That Half the Countries Intended for Introduction	
1 through 3		
	Bodies of water	Reproduction of organisms
	Weather and climate	Animal behavior
	Plants and fungi	Nutrition
	Animals	Disease
	Organs and tissues	Physical properties of matter
	Life cycles of organisms	Conservation of land, water, and sea resources
4 through 6		
	Composition	Interdependence of life
	Landforms	Classification of matter
	Atmosphere	Energy types, sources and conversions
	Rock and soil	Heat and temperature
	Physical cycles	Sound and vibration
	Building and breaking	Light
	Earth's history	Electricity
	Earth and the solar system	Magnetism
	Other organisms	Physical changes
	Cells	Time, space, and motion
	Energy handling	Pollution
	Biomes and ecosystems	Conservation of material and energy resources
	Habitats and niches	Effects of natural disasters
7 and 8		
	Ice forms	Chemical changes
	Beyond the solar system	Types of forces
	Sensing and responding	Dynamics of motion
	Variation and inheritances in organisms	Nature or conceptions of technology
	Evolution, speciation, and diversity	Applications of science in mathematics and technology
	Chemical properties of matter	History of science and technology
	Atoms, ions, and molecules	World population
	Subatomic particles	Food production and storage
	Explanations of physical changes	Nature of scientific nnowledge
9 through 12		
	Evolution of the universe	Organic and biochemical changes
	Biochemical processes in cells	Nuclear chemistry
	Biochemistry of genetics	Electrochemistry
	Macromolecules and crystals	Relativity theory
	Wave phenomena	Fluid behavior
	Kinetic theory	Influence of mathematics and technology in science
	Quantum theory and fundamental particles	Influence of science and technology on society
	Explanations of chemical changes	Influence of society on science and technology
	Rate of chemical change and equilibrium	Science and mathematics
	Energy and chemical change	

Source: Schmidt et al., 1997b, pp. 69-70.

QUESTIONS RELATED TO CURRICULAR FOCUS AND COHERENCE

- How many topics are covered in a given course or over an extended period in mathematics and science courses?
- How many topics are included in the textbooks used in mathematics and science courses? How are these topics related to each other within the text?
- What connections among topics exist within the curriculum? How are those connections made explicit to students from year to year, over the year, from topic to topic, from lesson to lesson, and within a single lesson? Should they be made more explicit; if so, how?
- What is the balance of time spent reviewing previously learned material and introducing new material?

---

structure of the curriculum along two interrelated dimensions: focus and coherence.

Focus

Focus in a curriculum measures the attention given to single topics either within single class sessions or across class sessions. (For a discussion of how topics were defined in TIMSS, see Schmidt et al., 1997c, pp. 127-130.) For example, in the draft *Principles and Standards for School Mathematics* developed by the National Council of Teachers of Mathematics (1998), the standards in each grade band are organized into discrete focus areas, such as "understanding the meaning of operations and how they relate to each other" under the number and operations standard, or "expressing mathematical ideas coherently and clearly to peers, teachers, and others" in the communication standard. The *Benchmarks for Science Literacy* produced by Project 2061 of the American Association for the Advancement of Science (1993) are organized into broad themes that emphasize "the common core of learning that contributes to the science literacy of all

students." Similarly, the *National Science Education Standards* (National Research Council, 1996) are organized into particular topics within content categories and grade bands, such as "position and movement of objects" within the physical science standard, or "science as a human endeavor" within the history and nature of science standard.

A strong impression conveyed by the TIMSS data is that other countries teach fewer content areas in any given year than does the United States (Schmidt et al., 1997c, pp. 1-11). At the same time, other countries appear to teach these subjects with greater depth and, as students progress through school, with greater rigor.

In the United States, in contrast, students cover more topics, but they seem to do so quickly and with a lack of higher levels of understanding. The potential disadvantage of teaching mathematics and science this way is the concept conveyed by the statement "more is less," implying that students exposed to a large number of disconnected topics tend to learn less overall than if the curriculum were more focused.

TIMSS offers several lines of evidence that point toward less focus in U.S. mathematics and science instruction compared to other countries. One involves the number of topics covered in U.S. mathematics and science textbooks. For populations 1 and 2, mathematics textbooks average 30 to 35 topics, compared with a median of 25 or fewer in other TIMSS countries (Figure 3-3). U.S. science textbooks contain even more topics—between 50 and 70 at the three student groupings studied in TIMSS, compared with an international median of between 20 and 30 (Figure 3-4). In fact, the number of topics in population 3 science and mathematics textbooks remains high despite the disciplinary orientation of curricula in high school.

The reasons for the large number of topics in mathematics and science textbooks differ somewhat between the two subjects. In science the number stems in part from the fact that there is no accepted sequence for the U.S.

curriculum. State curriculum guides have relatively limited overlap, which causes publishers—trying to gain maximum market share—to include many more topics in their textbooks than can be covered, much less learned.

In U.S. mathematics, on the other hand, there is a steady addition of topics according to well-accepted curriculum sequences, but—unlike elsewhere—few of the earlier topics are eliminated in later grades. This steady accumulation of topics is related to the emphasis on repetition and review in U.S. mathematics classes. U.S. textbooks tend to include many more review exercises and repeat more topics covered in earlier grades. Yet these texts offer little guidance on how or why to choose or eliminate topics, reflecting the absence of shared goals for mathematics learning (Schmidt et al., 1999, pp. 194-195).

Another measure of focus in textbooks involves the distribution of attention given to topics. Analyses of representative textbooks

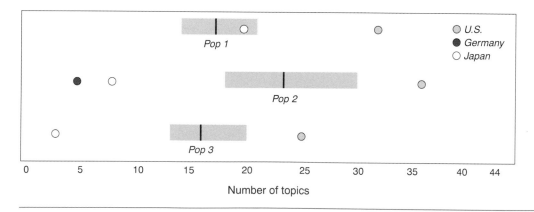

FIGURE 3-3 Number of topics in mathematics textbooks. The gray bars extend from the 25th percentile to the 75th percentile for the number of topics among countries studied in the TIMSS curriculum analysis. The black line within each gray bar indicates the median number of topics for each population. German textbook data were not available for populations 1 and 3. Source: Schmidt et al., 1997c, p. 55.

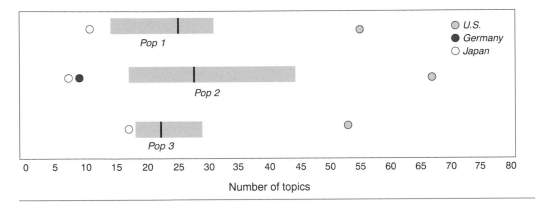

FIGURE 3-4 Number of topics in science textbooks. The gray bars extend from the 25th percentile to the 75th percentile for the number of topics among countries studied in the TIMSS curriculum analysis. The black line within each gray bar indicates the median number of topics for each population. German textbook data were not available for populations 1 and 3. Source: Schmidt et al., 1997c, p. 55.

found that the five topics emphasized most heavily in U.S. fourth-grade science textbooks accounted for just over 25 percent of the total material covered. In Japan the five most heavily emphasized topics accounted for 70 to 75 percent of the material (Figure 3-5).

The single-area textbooks commonly used in U.S. secondary schools would seem to offer greater focus. Here, too, however, the most emphasized five topics took up about 50 percent of the content, compared with an international average of 60 percent (Schmidt et al., 1997c, p. 61).

The number and organization of topics within textbooks are not necessarily related to the number of topics taught in a particular lesson or over the course of a year. Teachers can select topics from textbooks, or they can select textbooks that are more focused (the TIMSS curriculum analysis looked at the broad range of textbooks available in different countries

without trying to calculate their popularity or market share). The composite curriculum represented in textbooks may appear to be unfocused without implying that a given student's curriculum is unfocused.

However, other data collected during TIMSS similarly point toward a comparatively superficial treatment of a large number of topics in U.S. mathematics and science classrooms. For example, when eighth-grade U.S. mathematics and science teachers were asked in questionnaires to identify which topics they taught over the course of a year, far more reported teaching a large number of topics than was the case in Japan or Germany (Schmidt et al., 1997c, pp. 69-72). They also reported devoting less than half their time to the five most highly covered topics, indicating that teachers' instructional time is as inclusive and unfocused as the structure of typical U.S. textbooks.

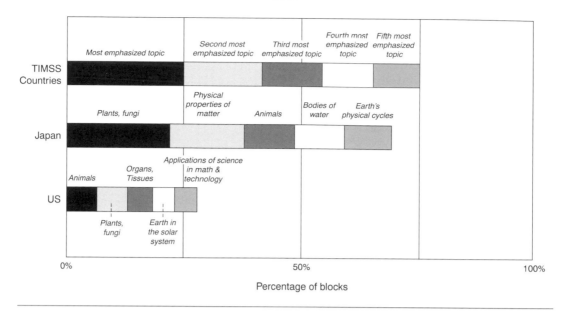

FIGURE 3-5 The five topics emphasized most in population 1 science textbooks. Source: Schmidt et al., 1997c, p. 58.

Coherence

Closely related to the number of topics in mathematics and science classes is the relationship of topics to each other within and across classes—a quality referred to in this report by the term "coherence." Coherence is a measure of the connectedness of the mathematics and science ideas and skills presented to students over an extended period of time. A coherent curriculum can be thought of as a smoothly developing story in science and mathematics. In a coherent curriculum, new or more complex ideas and skills build on previous learning, applications are used to reinforce prior learning, and extensive repetition is avoided.

The national standards in both mathematics and science emphasize the need for coherence. In the draft *Principles and Standards for School Mathematics* (National Council of Teachers of Mathematics, 1998), the same standards and focus areas extend across all grades, from pre-kindergarten through twelfth grade, providing a potential coherence across a student's schooling. The broad content standards of the *National Science Education Standards* (National Research Council, 1996) and *Benchmarks for Science Literacy* (American Association for the Advancement of Science, 1993) also extend across all grades, allowing teachers at each level to build on previously learned knowledge and skills.

Furthermore, both sets of standards emphasize the need for coherence between the two disciplines. The science standards list as one of the program standards that: "The science program should be coordinated with the mathematics program to enhance student use and understanding of mathematics in the study of science and to improve student understanding of mathematics" (National Research Council, 1996, p. 214). The draft mathematics standards state, "Of all disciplines, science probably has the most obvious connections with mathematics. The link between mathematics and science is not only through content, but also through process. The processes and content of science can inspire an approach to solving problems that applies to the study of mathematics" (National Council of Teachers of Mathematics, 1998, p. 93).

Several observations made by TIMSS demonstrate serious threats to coherence in U.S. mathematics and science curricula. First, the organization of topics within texts suggests that they are not well connected (though it does not prove that they are not well connected). Consider, for example, a schematic portrait of a Japanese versus a U.S. mathematics textbook (Figure 3-6). In the Japanese textbook, eight topics are organized into long sequences. The U.S. textbook has many more topics widely scattered across class sessions.

The videotapes of eighth-grade mathematics also point to a lack of coherence in U.S. lessons (Stigler et al., 1999, pp. 46-47). The videotape studies showed that U.S. lessons contained significantly more topics than did Japanese lessons and that U.S. teachers made significantly more switches from topic to topic than did German or Japanese teachers (Figure 3-7).

One way to help students perceive the coherence of ideas is explicitly to point out the connections among them. In the video study of eighth-grade mathematics, a number of lessons (15 from geometry and 15 from algebra) were randomly chosen from each country and all of the verbal statements made by the teachers were coded. Those lessons that contained at least one concrete statement that connected the current idea to ideas or events in another part

of the lesson or to ideas in another lesson were identified. The majority of teachers in all countries made explicit links from one lesson to another. Only about 40 percent of German and U.S. teachers made links between parts of a lesson, compared with 96 percent of Japanese teachers (Stigler et al., 1999, pp. 117-118).

Some judgments about coherence, such as the flow of mathematical connections, require a good deal of sophistication about teaching mathematics. The videotape study of TIMSS therefore had a group of four university mathematics teachers (the Math Group) analyze a sample of the videotaped lessons. The Math Group worked from written descriptions of the lessons, with references to specific countries disguised, so that they did not know the origin of a particular lesson.

Using the same 15 geometry and 15 algebra lessons from each country used for coding the teachers' verbal behavior, the Math Group devised a means of systematically describing the mathematical content of each lesson along dimensions they thought were relevant for student learning. (This method is described in detail in Stigler et al., 1999, pp. 58-61.) The group isolated the lesson segments, the connections among those segments, and the kinds of relationships that characterized the connections. They then measured the coherence of lessons by determining which segments were connected through at least one appropriate mathematical relationship, such as one segment was helpful for the next or two segments were similar. Of the 30 lessons analyzed from each country, 45 percent of the U.S. lessons, 76 percent of the German lessons, and 92 percent of the Japanese lessons fit this criterion of coherence.

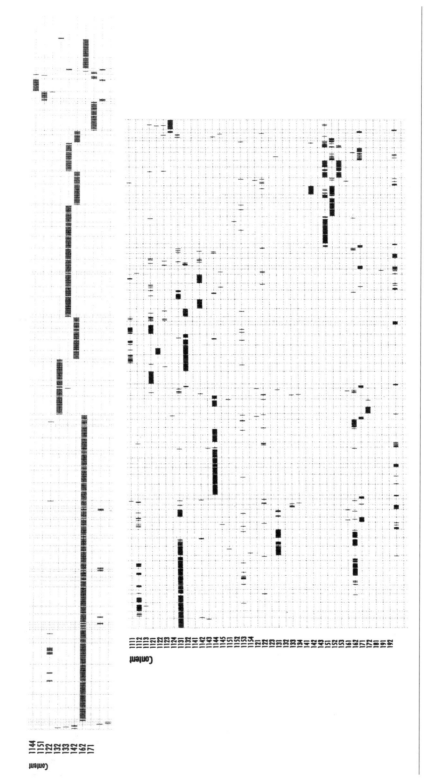

FIGURE 3-6 Schematic overview of population 2 mathematics textbooks from Japan and the United States. Each small vertical dash represents a single unit of analysis within the textbook, such as a single discussion, problem, or task. The dashes are organized into rows corresponding to the TIMSS mathematics curriculum framework (the numbers labeled "content" refer to specific topic areas). Thus, columns refer to units of analysis and rows to topic areas. The Japanese textbook covers a limited number of topics with infrequent switches among topics. The U.S. textbook, in contrast, covers many more topics than does the Japanese text (indicated by the greater number of content areas) and does so in a less continuous fashion. The analysis shown here for the U.S. text covers only about one quarter of the entire book, which is why some content areas are not covered. Source: Schmidt et al., 1997c, pp. 99-101.

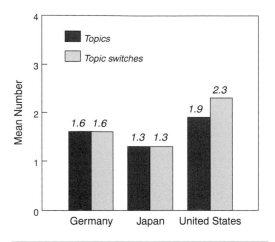

FIGURE 3-7 Average number of topics and topic switches per videotaped lesson in Germany, Japan, and the United States. Source: Stigler et al., 1999, p. 47.

Lesson coherence is about more than just telling a single story because single mathematical stories can be told simply by working through a series of similar problems. Rich coherence comes from artfully piecing together segments, creating tensions and dilemmas, and building toward a conclusion. The Math Group tried to capture this distinction by looking for a variety of mathematical relationships among segments of lessons. By adding all of the ways segments were mathematically related, they produced an estimate of how richly a lesson was connected. Using this measure, U.S. lessons were much less coherent than those in Germany and Japan.

Finally, in addition to analyzing specific features of the lessons, the Math Group assessed the overall quality of the mathematics in each lesson with regard to its potential for helping students understand important mathematics. This subjective judgment was, of course, related

to coherence, but it also took into account other aspects of mathematics, such as the level of challenge and how the content was developed. Using these subjective measures, the Math Group sorted the lessons into three content quality categories: low, medium, and high. In the judgment of these experienced mathematics teachers, U.S. students were at a clear disadvantage in their opportunities to learn, at least as indicated by the content to which they were exposed (Figure 3-8).

The lack of coherence in U.S. eighth-grade mathematics classes reinforces the conclusions made earlier in this chapter about the unfocused nature of U.S. curricula in mathematics and science. Without a clear set of goals that can establish connections among topics—goals such as those provided by national, state, and local standards in mathematics and science—it can be difficult to construct coherent mathematical and scientific stories in classes that cover a large number of topics.

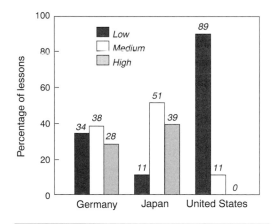

FIGURE 3-8 Percentage of lessons rated as having low, medium, and high quality of mathematical content. The total for Japan adds to more than 100 because of rounding. Source: Stigler et al., 1999, p. 70.

CHAPTER FOUR

What Does TIMSS Say About Instructional Practices?

Science and mathematics teachers around the world face many similar challenges (Robitaille, 1997, p. 32). Most teach classes of about 30 students in lesson blocks that are a little less or a little more than an hour. They generally have a particular curriculum they intend to cover during a course. They want students to acquire certain competencies.

Teachers around the world also have similar concerns. According to data gathered by TIMSS, many teachers believe that high student-to-teacher ratios limit their ability to teach. Many teachers report shortages of equipment for use in demonstrations and other exercises. In the large majority of TIMSS countries, disruptive students, differences in academic abilities, and unmotivated students are cited by many teachers as factors that limit their ability to teach (Martin et al., 1997, pp. 141-143).

How do teachers and educational systems around the world deal with these common challenges and concerns? The results of TIMSS show that teachers and systems in different countries tend to solve similar problems in different ways. In turn, these solutions often reflect the beliefs and assumptions that teachers—and those who influence teachers—hold about teaching and learning.

This chapter discusses what teachers actually *do* in the classroom and the reasons behind their actions. It does not address the broader context for teaching and learning, such as teacher preparation and student attitudes (these and other topics are covered in the following chapter). Rather, by examining how teachers in other countries attempt to solve common problems of practice, this chapter presents options for instructional practices in the United States that might not otherwise be considered.

The national standards in both mathematics and science cite the critical importance of teachers' knowledge, understanding, and skills in mathematics and science learning. According to the *National Science Education Standards* (National Research Council, 1996, p. 28), "Effective teaching is at the heart of science education. . . . The decisions about content and activities that teachers make, their interactions with students, the selection of assessments, the habits of mind that teachers demonstrate and nurture among their students, and the attitudes conveyed wittingly and unwittingly all affect the knowledge, understanding, abilities, and attitudes that students develop."

The *Professional Standards for Teaching Mathematics* (National Council of Teachers of Mathematics, 1991, p. 22) point out that "teaching is a complex practice and hence not reducible to recipes or prescriptions." Teachers must draw on many kinds of knowledge in the classroom while adapting their teaching to particular students and contexts. They also have to balance multiple goals in deciding what and how to teach. And teachers work within an administrative and cultural context that shapes their actions. Good practice in teaching cannot be prescribed but must emerge from a teacher's knowledge, judgment, and circumstances.

The first section of this chapter discusses some of the variations in instructional practice that emerge from varying circumstances, such as the activities in which students are engaged in mathematics and science classes and how much homework they are assigned. The second part of the chapter probes beneath these specific activities by examining some of the key influences on instructional practices, including the learning goals that teachers hold for students and their beliefs about teaching. The chapter concludes with descriptions and commentary for two sample lessons, one from the United States and one from Japan, demonstrating common teaching practices in each country. As in the previous chapter and the next chapter, questions at the beginning of each major section provide guides for considering educational changes in light of the results from TIMSS.

The information presented in this chapter comes from two main sources: the TIMSS background questionnaires given to administrators, teachers, and students and the video study of eighth-grade mathematics teaching in Germany, Japan, and the United States. It can be difficult to use survey data to illuminate an activity as complex as teaching, but the TIMSS questionnaires probed a wide range of beliefs, attitudes, and practices. The videotapes, in contrast, provide vivid impressions of what happens in classrooms but are less revealing about the motivations and thinking processes of teachers. (The videotape analysis also looked only at mathematics and only at the eighth grade.) Together, the two sources of data provide complementary insights into teaching practices.

VARIATIONS IN INSTRUCTIONAL PRACTICE

Lesson Structure

Teachers at the fourth- and eighth-grade levels who participated in TIMSS filled out questionnaires asking how much class time they spent on a number of different instructional practices. This analysis revealed that lesson structure has some common features among countries, though interesting differences also appeared.

The two most common activities in U.S. mathematics teachers' classrooms at the fourth-

and eighth-grade levels are teachers working with the whole class and students working individually with assistance from the teacher (Beaton et al., 1996a, pp. 151-155; Mullis et al., 1997, pp. 162-166). These two activities are also the most common internationally.

An exception to the predominance of these two activities can be found in fourth-grade science in the United States, where the second most common practice is for the class to work together as a whole with students responding to each other. This also is true in Japan, Korea, and the Netherlands (Martin et al., 1997, pp. 145-147), but it is not the case in eighth-grade science in the United States (Beaton et al., 1996b, pp. 143-147).

The questionnaire on instructional practices also produced information on the amount of review and new material that students received in mathematics and science classes. According to this analysis, more than half of U.S. eighth-grade mathematics students received fewer than 20 minutes of instruction on new material in a typical 50-minute class period. Instruction on

---

QUESTIONS RELATED TO VARIATIONS IN INSTRUCTIONAL PRACTICE

- How are mathematics and science lessons typically structured? Does classwork, seatwork, or some other instructional practice dominate individual lessons?
- How much new material is presented and how much review occurs in each class?
- Who is more responsible for developing and drawing connections among mathematical and scientific ideas—students or the teacher?
- How complex are the exercises undertaken by students? How often are students asked to engage in deductive reasoning?
- How much time do students spend practicing routine procedures, applying concepts, and inventing new solutions or approaches during both classwork and seatwork?
- What is the testing schedule for mathematics and science? Do tests and quizzes reinforce a deeper understanding of mathematics and science?
- How much homework is given per day, and how much of this homework is done during class time? How does the time spent working on homework during the lesson extend student understanding?

new material was somewhat more frequent in science; 43.5 percent of U.S. eighth-grade science teachers provided 20 minutes or more of such material in each class (Schmidt et al., 1999, pp. 65-67). Both internationally and in the United States, review was a more dominant instructional practice for mathematics than for science.

The videotape studies of eighth-grade mathematics in Japan, Germany, and the United States substantiate these findings (Stigler and Hiebert, 1997; Stigler et al., 1999). These data reveal that teachers in all three countries spend more time doing classwork, where the teacher works with the entire class, than seatwork, where students work on their own or in small groups. However, shifts within the lesson from classwork to seatwork and vice versa were considerably more frequent in Japan than in the other two countries. As a result, the duration of segments defined by teaching practices tended to be shorter in Japan than in the other countries, giving the lessons a more punctuated feel.

An important finding from the videotape studies relates to whether teachers or students are doing the bulk of the mathematical work. Most classroom time in all three countries was devoted to setting up tasks, working on tasks, and sharing solutions or correcting tasks either during classwork or seatwork. If a task is done during classwork, teachers are often doing much of the work. If it is done during seatwork, students are more likely to be doing the work. The videotape analysis shows that Japanese classes spent more time working on tasks during seatwork than during classwork, whereas the reverse was true in Germany (Figure 4-1). U.S. classes divided the work equally between classwork and seatwork.

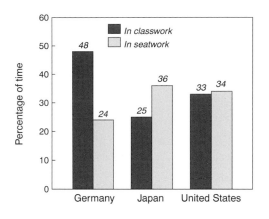

FIGURE 4-1 Average percentage of lesson time spent working on tasks during classwork and seatwork. Source: Stigler et al., 1999, p. 87.

The three countries also differed in the complexity of the exercises undertaken by students (Manaster, 1998). In Japan, multistep tasks were most common, occurring in 90 percent of lessons. In the United States and Germany, multistep tasks were found in 62 and 63 percent of lessons, respectively.

The three countries differed starkly in how often the videotapes showed explicit instances of mathematical reasoning (Manaster, 1998). In Japan, 53 percent of lessons had clear instances of reasoning. In Germany, 20 percent of lessons indicated that mathematical reasoning had taken place. In the United States, however, none of the videotaped lessons presented evidence of reasoning in mathematics.

Perhaps the best way to measure student engagement in mathematics is to assess the kind of mathematical activity in which students are engaged during seatwork. Seatwork tasks in the videotaped classes were coded into three categories: practicing routine procedures, applying concepts or procedures in new

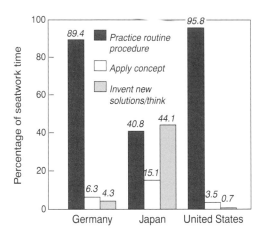

FIGURE 4-2 Average percentage of seatwork time spent practicing routine procedures, applying concepts, or thinking and inventing new solutions. Source: Stigler et al., 1999, p. 102.

situations, and inventing something new or analyzing situations in new ways. In this analysis, Japan differed significantly from the United States and Germany (Figure 4-2). Japanese students spent about the same amount of time practicing routine procedures and inventing something new, whereas German and U.S. students spent almost all of their time practicing routine procedures.

Calculators and Computers

U.S. teachers indicated in TIMSS that they use calculators and computers as much as or more than teachers in most other countries. At the population 1 level in mathematics, 39 percent reported using calculators once or twice a week, versus an international average of 18 percent (U.S. Department of Eduation, 1997b, p. 42). Although calculators are almost universally available in the TIMSS countries, teachers

in some countries (including high and low performers) reported never or hardly ever having students use calculators.

At population 2, both teachers and students in a majority of countries reported using calculators pretty often or almost every day in mathematics (Beaton et al., 1996a, pp. 162-168). However, in some countries, including some high-achieving countries (such as Japan and Korea) as well as in some low-achieving countries, mathematics teachers rarely had students use calculators.

Students at the high school level were given the opportunity to use calculators during the assessments of mathematics and science general knowledge in TIMSS. A smaller proportion of U.S. students did so than the international average—71 to 79 percent (U.S. Department of Education, 1998, p. 66).

The United States was one of a quarter of TIMSS countries where 50 to 75 percent of population 1 students had computers at home (Mullis et al., 1997, p. 114). Computers were not used often in U.S. mathematics or science classes by populations 1 or 2, but even this infrequent use surpassed that in most countries.

Among the U.S. physics and advanced mathematics students, 42 percent reported use of computers in some, most, or every lesson (Mullis et al., 1998, pp. 169, 225). This is comparable to the international average, although it is much more frequent than in some countries (e.g., Austria, France, and Germany).

Tests, Quizzes, and External Examinations

U.S. mathematics and science teachers rely heavily on tests and quizzes in the eighth grade, which was the only population at which TIMSS collected extensive data on assessment practices. For example, 85 percent of U.S. eighth-grade mathematics students report that their teachers "pretty often" or "almost always" use tests and quizzes (Beaton et al., 1996a, pp. 172-175). The combined percentage is higher than that reported in any other TIMSS country.

Tests and quizzes in the United States also played a large role in teachers' reports to parents. Among the 38 countries that provided these data at the population 2 level, the United States was one of only five where 80 percent or more of eighth-grade students were taught by teachers who used assessments for this purpose (Beaton et al., 1996a, p. 174).

The effect of external assessments, such as standardized tests and college entrance examinations, on classroom practices was not investigated directly in TIMSS. Nevertheless, these assessments can be assumed to have a substantial impact. In many foreign countries, for example, most major external examinations, and especially those affecting access to different forms of postsecondary education, consist wholly or mostly of items that require extended student responses. Given the enormous impact of these examinations on students' lives, teachers want to be sure their students are prepared for them. It seems reasonable, therefore, that teachers would put a premium on providing instruction that increases students' proficiency in writing extended responses.

Homework

U.S. elementary and middle school teachers seem to assign amounts of homework comparable to teachers in other countries. U.S. fourth-grade teachers typically assign 30 minutes or less of mathematics homework three or more days per week (U.S. Department of Education, 1997b, p. 40). U.S. eighth graders typically spend between a half hour and an hour studying mathematics and science outside school each day (U.S. Department of Education, 1996, p. 63).

At grade 12 the general U.S. student population reports doing considerably less homework overall than students in their final year of secondary school in other countries—1.7 hours per day on all subjects versus 2.6 hours per day for the international average (U.S. Department of Education, 1998, p. 65). U.S. students taking a mathematics or science course reported doing about as much homework in these subjects as students in other countries in their last year of secondary school.

Among students taking advanced mathematics or physics, a much higher percentage of U.S. students report having homework three or more times per week than students in other countries—90 versus 66 percent for advanced mathematics students, and 50 versus 40 percent for physics students (U.S. Department of Education, 1998, p. 74).

Comparisons of homework are complicated by differing meanings for the term. In the United States, homework typically means any educational activity that could be conducted outside school (even if that activity takes place inside school). Homework can mean studying for class tests, doing independent projects, preparing for important external examinations such as college entrance exams, or optional work meant to provide further understanding. In some other countries, teachers, parents, and students tend to make more of a distinction between homework and studying. In those countries, for example, homework might not include studying for external exams.

The United States is one of very few countries where teachers frequently assign homework that students actually begin during class time. U.S. teachers are almost alone in allocating considerable class time to work on homework—something that foreign researchers found very surprising during the development of TIMSS.

INFLUENCES ON INSTRUCTIONAL PRACTICES

Beneath the observable activities that occur in mathematics and science classes are the external forces and internal motivations that influence instruction in particular ways. Some of these influences are embedded in the curriculum, as described in the previous chapter. Others constitute part of the support systems available to schools, teachers, and students—the subject of the next chapter. The next major section of this chapter describes the information provided by TIMSS on four particularly important factors that affect teaching: decisions about what to teach, lesson objectives, teachers' beliefs about instruction, and the "scripts" that shape teaching. At the end of the chapter, a description of classrooms in two different countries demonstrates how these influences shape teaching.

Deciding What to Teach

When teachers were asked in questionnaires, "What is your main source in deciding which topics to teach?," the most frequent response from U.S. teachers, for both populations 1 and 2 and in both subjects, was the "National Curriculum Guide." This response is somewhat difficult to interpret, since the United States does not have a national curriculum guide. It seems likely, however, that teachers were referring to the national standards and benchmarks in mathematics and science, which would indicate a widespread awareness of those documents. (At the time the questionnaires

---

QUESTIONS RELATED TO INFLUENCES ON INSTRUCTIONAL PRACTICES

• Who has the authority over curricular and instructional decisions in mathematics and science? Should this authority be redistributed in any way? If so, to whom should authority be redistributed and why?

• How are beliefs about science and mathematics learning connected to the way these subjects are taught? Are there reasons to change prevailing beliefs? If beliefs do need to be changed, what are the most effective ways of doing so?

• How much freedom are students given to explore their own solution methods to problems? If they were allowed more freedom, what might result?

• What are the prevailing "scripts" for teaching mathematics? What role does computation play in those scripts? To what extent do scripts make change difficult?

• How do scripts for teaching science in the United States differ from those for teaching mathematics?

• How could scripts for teaching in the United States be rewritten to better serve valued ends of education? Can students and teachers adjust to new scripts?

were distributed, the *Benchmarks for Science Literacy* produced by Project 2061 of the American Association for the Advancement of Science were available, though the *National Science Education Standards* from the National Research Council were still in draft form.)

In contrast, teachers in Japan, a country that does have a national curriculum guide, selected the teachers' edition of the text as most influential in deciding what to teach. Part of the explanation for this choice probably is that approved textbook series in Japan follow the national curriculum, and many teachers' manuals in Japan are developed by the teachers themselves and contain rich information for planning lessons. Teachers in Japan may believe that following the teachers' manual both satisfies the national guidelines and provides pedagogical help.

Another item on the teacher questionnaire asked what resources teachers rely on to decide how to present a topic. Perhaps the most interesting result was that many teachers in many countries selected the teachers' edition of the text and the student text. This finding is not surprising in the United States, given previous research showing teachers' reliance on the text. It is interesting that teachers in many other countries responded in similar ways.

Another question, which was asked of the principal of the school, was: "In your school, who has primary responsibility for choosing textbooks?" According to the principals, teachers in the United States have a greater voice in choosing textbooks than in the Asian comparison countries and almost as great a voice as in the European countries. In Japan this is generally not a school responsibility, and

in Singapore the principal or department head usually chooses the text. In European countries, choosing a textbook is usually a school affair and often the teachers' responsibility. In some schools, however, the responsibility rests with the principal and in others with the department head.

Another question asked of principals was: "In your school, who has primary responsibility for determining course content?" Again, according to school principals, teachers in the United States have considerable influence in choosing content. The responses to this question, however, should be interpreted with caution. In some countries, determining the course content appears to be less of a school responsibility than choosing the textbook. Perhaps this is because the respondents believed that, once the text is chosen, the content is determined.

One interesting aspect of the responses from both teachers and principals was the rating of the district school board as quite influential in determining course content and curriculum in the United States. In most other countries a comparable entity did not exist.

To greatly simplify the issue of curricular choice and autonomy, it appears that the high-achieving countries in TIMSS place the greatest control in the hands of educational experts, either national leaders (e.g., in Japan or Singapore) or classroom teachers (e.g., in the Czech Republic and the Netherlands). The United States introduces a third influence—a middle-level agency, the district school board, composed of individuals who do not work full time in education and generally are not professionally trained in the field.

Objectives of Lessons

Teachers' goals are reflected in the skills and knowledge they seek to impart in lessons. One valuable source of information about these goals are the videotapes made of eighth-grade mathematics classes. Although these videotapes focus on just a single subject at a single grade level, and although statements about patterns inevitably overgeneralize the data, the observed patterns do summarize the interpretations of the researchers who coded the videotapes.

In Germany the teacher is clearly in charge of determining the mathematical content, and the mathematics is quite advanced, at least procedurally. In many lessons the teacher leads the students through a development of procedures for solving general classes of problems. There is a concern for technique, where technique includes both the rationale that underlies the procedures and the precision with which the procedure is executed. A good general description of German mathematics teaching at this level would be "developing advanced procedures."

In Japan the teacher appears to take a less active role, allowing students to invent their own strategies for solving problems. The problems are quite demanding, both procedurally and conceptually. The teacher, however, carefully designs and orchestrates the lesson so that students are likely to use procedures recently developed in class. An appropriate description of Japanese teaching in mathematics would be "structured problem solving."

In the United States the content is less advanced and requires less mathematical reasoning than in the other two countries.

Tasks presented to students are less complex, and their solution is less commonly controlled by the student. The teacher presents definitions of terms and demonstrates procedures for solving specific problems, and students are asked to memorize the definitions and practice the procedures. In the United States the general description of eighth-grade mathematics teaching could be "learning terms and practicing procedures."

In Germany and the United States, students engage in mathematics by following the teacher's lead. In Germany this often takes the form of responding to specific questions from the teacher as the whole class develops a relatively advanced procedure. In the United States this often takes the form of following the teacher's directions by practicing relatively simple procedures during seatwork.

Although it may be tempting to say that the reverse is true in Japan—that students control the mathematics—the data indicate that this is not the case. A more accurate picture is that, on average, there is a balance in Japan. The mathematical work is shared by the teacher and the students. Students sometimes, but not always, do creative mathematical work by inventing new methods and presenting them to the class. At other times, teachers control the mathematics—lecturing, demonstrating, asking students to memorize, and so on. The Japanese practice of lesson study, in which groups of teachers come together to study and improve the teaching of particular lessons, helps teachers understand what their students are capable of doing and provides them with knowledge they can use to teach more effectively (Stigler and Hiebert, 1999).

Beliefs About Mathematics Teaching

Based on analysis of the videotapes, teachers in different countries seem to have different beliefs about the nature of mathematics. Although highly inferential, the following observations are consistent with the majority of the videotaped lessons and the responses of videotaped teachers on the questionnaire.

In general, teachers in the United States say that students' success in mathematics is related to their ability to "understand" concepts. However, the typical U.S. lesson is consistent with the belief that school mathematics is a set of skills. In fact, 61 percent of teachers said that the main thing they wanted students to learn from the videotaped lesson was how to perform a particular operation or to acquire a particular skill. Apparently, there is a mismatch between what teachers say is most important for students and the goals they set for individual lessons.

According to the psychology of learning that seems to dominate many U.S. classrooms, skills arc learned best by mastering material incrementally, piece by piece. The best learning conditions therefore involve practicing each piece, with high levels of success at each step. Confusion and frustration are taken by teachers as signs that the earlier material was not mastered. This means that the teacher's role is to divide the task into pieces that are manageable, providing all the information needed to complete the task, and providing plenty of practice. Providing information means, to many teachers, demonstrating how to complete a task like those assigned.

In contrast, the typical Japanese lesson seems to be based on a different psychology of learning—one in which students learn best through a variety of activities, including struggling with a problem and *then* participating in the discussion about how to solve it. Confusion and frustration are seen as a natural part of the process and are used to prepare the student for the information received during the discussion. The teacher's role is to choose a problem that engages students and will reveal the mathematics of interest and to help students understand the problem so they can begin their attempts to solve it. The teacher then manages the discussion such that different methods get heard, and the teacher summarizes the relationships of interest at the conclusion. In addition, the teacher needs to provide information and opportunities for practice when these are needed to construct the intended relationships.

Teaching Scripts

To gain a deeper appreciation for how countries differ in science and mathematics instruction, it is useful to think about instructional differences not just as arbitrary collections of teaching techniques but as unified "scripts" for teaching. These scripts draw on the elements and aspects of instruction described above, including goals for instruction, beliefs about the nature of science and mathematics, beliefs about how those subjects are learned and should be taught, and the characteristics of a normal or typical lesson.

Because TIMSS gathered more information about mathematics instruction than about science instruction, it provides a clearer picture of scripts for the teaching of mathematics than for the teaching of science. These scripts represent, in some sense, abstractions of the recurring features illustrated in the sample lessons. In brief, the U.S. script for eighth-grade mathematics seems to have four basic components: (1) the teacher reviews previous material (often by checking homework), (2) the teacher demonstrates how to solve that day's problems, (3) students practice (usually individually on assigned seatwork), and (4) the teacher corrects practice problems and assigns homework.

The most instructive contrasts in national teaching scripts can be found in Japan. In Japanese mathematics classes, (1) the teacher reviews previous material (usually by giving a brief lecture or asking students questions), (2) the teacher presents problems for the day, (3) students work on problems (usually for a set number of minutes individually, then sometimes in small groups), (4) the whole class discusses solution methods (often the teacher selects students to share their work based on what he or she has seen while circulating around the class), and (5) the teacher highlights and summarizes major points.

Instructional reform, especially if it involves borrowing from other countries and cultures, needs to appreciate how these scripts are deeply embedded in the culture of their originating country and, in fact, constitute cultures of teaching in their own right. Learning from TIMSS means, in part, appreciating one's individual and collective scripts for teaching science and mathematics and understanding the scripts used by teachers around the world. Focusing on the differences among potential scripts during preservice and ongoing teacher education provides one way in which scripts

could be changed or "rewritten." Such rewriting is not necessarily easy, but it becomes possible as insight is gained into how science and mathematics teaching varies among countries and among teachers.

INSTRUCTIONAL PRACTICES AND THE STANDARDS

The national mathematics and science standards call for forms of teaching quite different from what is found in many U.S. classrooms. The teaching described in the standards treats learning as an active process. For example, in the classes described in the science standards, students "describe objects and events, ask questions, construct explanations, test those explanations against current scientific knowledge, and communicate their ideas to others" (National Research Council, 1996, p. 2). In standards-based mathematics classes it is assumed "that students should be exposed to numerous and varied interrelated experiences that encourage them to value the mathematical enterprise, to develop mathematical habits of mind, and to understand and appreciate the role of mathematics in humans affairs; that they should be encouraged to explore, to guess, and even to make and correct errors so that they gain confidence in their ability to solve complex problems; that they should read, write, and discuss mathematics; and that they should conjecture, test, and build arguments about a conjecture's validity" (National Council of Teachers of Mathematics, 1989, p. 5).

This report does not lay out specific recommendations designed to move instructional practice toward the goals laid out in the national standards documents. However, the descriptions of teaching presented in this chapter do highlight one aspect of reform: changing instructional practices in the United States will require reexamining deep-seated beliefs about teaching and learning. As the *National Science Education Standards* point out, "All teachers . . . have implicit and explicit beliefs about science, learning, and teaching. Teachers can be effective guides for students learning science only if they have the opportunity to examine their own beliefs" (p. 28). Similarly, the draft *Principles and Standards for School Mathematics* states that "teachers can provide classrooms that promote thinking, but it takes much more than worthwhile mathematical tasks and a commitment to discourse. It takes deep insight about mathematics, about teaching, and about learners, coupled with a sound and robust mathematics curriculum and thoughtful reflection and planning" (p. 33).

This chapter concludes with descriptions of two classrooms, one in the United States and one in Japan, that demonstrate many of the common features of mathematics teaching in those two countries. These descriptions point to both the potential and the challenges in moving toward standards-based instructional practices.

SAMPLE EIGHTH-GRADE MATHEMATICS LESSONS IN THE UNITED STATES AND JAPAN

The following material describes "typical" U.S. eighth-grade mathematics lessons in the United States and Japan videotaped as part of TIMSS. It is not easy to decide that a specific lesson is typical, given the complexity of the lessons and the variations in each country. Nevertheless, the lessons as a whole reveal certain general patterns, and the following lessons, which focus on geometry, illustrate many of these patterns. These lessons are described in more detail in the book *The Teaching Gap* by James Stigler and James Hiebert (New York: Free Press, 1999).

A U.S. LESSON

Reviewing Previous Material and Checking Homework

The video begins with Mr. Jones, the teacher, conducting a "warm-up" activity. He points to the top left-hand drawing on the chalkboard.

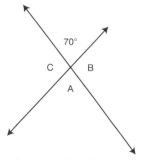

Mr. Jones:	What is the angle vertical to the 70 degree angle? (Pause) John?
John:	I don't know.
Mr. Jones:	When I intersect lines I get vertical angles. Right? Look at your definition. I gave them to you. You can look them up. Here we have vertical angles and supplementary angles. Angle A is vertical to which angle?
Students:	Seventy (in chorus).
Mr. Jones:	Therefore, angle A must be?
Students:	Seventy degrees (in chorus).
Mr. Jones:	Seventy degrees. Go from there. Now you have supplementary angles, don't you? What angle is supplementary to angle B?

After five minutes of this quick-paced review, Mr. Jones asks the students to "get out the worksheet I gave [you] earlier in the week and make sure we understand complementary, supplementary, and angle measurements." The class goes over the worksheet in a similar way: Mr. Jones asks students for answers and questions them when they are wrong. For example:

Mr. Jones: What is the complement of an angle of 7 degrees, Jose?
Jose: Eighty-three.
Mr. Jones: Eighty-three. The complement of an angle of 84, Marsha, would be?
Marsha: Sixteen.
Mr. Jones: Are you sure about your arithmetic on that one?
Marsha: Six?
Mr. Jones: Six. Six degrees. Bob, number four.

The class checks 36 problems on the worksheet during six minutes of similar question/answer interaction. For the last few problems, Mr. Jones draws the picture of two congruent triangles on the chalkboard, positioned as mirror images of each other. The task is to match up the congruent parts of the triangle, and Mr. Jones checks that students completed each of these correctly, emphasizing the notation that is used to label line segments, angles, and congruence.

The patterns for eighth-grade mathematics instruction in the United States are evident—get the terms and definitions straight and learn the procedures for solving specific kinds of problems. The nature and level of the mathematics also are quite simple compared with those found in typical Japanese and German lessons. The opening activities are typical as well—many lessons in the United States begin with warm-up activities, checking homework, or both.

Demonstrating Procedures

Next Mr. Jones distributes a worksheet that contains problems that, he notes, are "just like the warm-up." At the top of the worksheet is a sample problem with the solution and a suggested method shown. Mr. Jones goes over this with the students.

Mr. Jones: (Referring to the angles in the drawing) One and three are vertical.
              Two and four are vertical. Two and three are supplementary. So if
              three is 120, what must two be equal to?

Roxanne:	Sixty?
Mr. Jones:	Sixty. If two is 60, what must four be equal to?
Students:	Sixty (in chorus).
Mr. Jones:	Okay. All the rest are done the same way. Any questions? I'm curious to see, when you get down to 37 and 38, you're going to have to think a little bit. Curious to see what you can come up with on those.

Practicing the Procedures

The worksheet contains 40 problems and the students spend the next 11 minutes working on them. The problems, like the homework and the warm-up, emphasize terms and procedures. Mr. Jones circulates around the room, answering questions and giving hints. So far the lesson is unfolding like many lessons in the United States. Procedures are demonstrated, students practice the procedures on similar problems, and the teacher moves around the room to tutor individual students who need help.

Mr. Jones starts receiving questions about numbers 37 and 38 and initiates a class discussion about these problems.

Mr. Jones:	Has anyone come up knowing that the product means multiplication? Has anyone come up with the answer to number 38? (The problem, listed under "Spiral Review" on the worksheet, says, "Write an equation that represents the sentence: The product of 12 and a number k is 192.")
Students:	(Mixed chorus of no and yes).
Mr. Jones:	What did you get, Cynthia?
Cynthia:	(Confused).
Mr. Jones:	Twelve and k. (Begins to write on the chalkboard $12k$ and then says slowly) . . . is 192.
Cynthia:	Equal sign.
Mr. Jones:	Excellent (fills in "= 192").
Joshua:	That's it?
Mr. Jones:	That's it. Doesn't it say that the product of 12 and the number k is 192?

It may strike the reader that this task has nothing to do with today's lesson, but some U.S. commercial materials include review of earlier topics in later problem sets. In fact, it is not uncommon to find this kind of topic switch during U.S. lessons.

Demonstrating More Procedures

Mr. Jones gives the students two more minutes to finish the worksheet and then asks them to get out the worksheet they completed last Friday after the quiz. He goes over two problems with them, both involving measuring angles using a protractor. The second problem begins by measuring the interior angles of a hexagon, shown below, and computing the total. Mr. Jones asks if everyone got close to 720 degrees. He then proceeds to the second part of the problem.

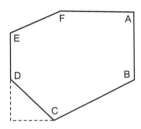

Mr. Jones:	If I took this angle (D) and moved it down here and made it across this way (see dotted lined in drawing). Moved D down here, should that change the sum, the total?
Jason:	No. (Other students add "no.")
Mr. Jones:	It should not. Why? I still have how many angles?
Obed:	You still have six.
Mr. Jones:	I still have six angles. There is a formula, and we are going to go through this after spring break, but I will give you a hint right now. If I take the number of sides and I subtract two, and I multiply that number times 180 degrees, that will tell me how many degrees these add up to. How many sides in this figure? (Pause) Six. Right? Number of sides subtract two, gives me what?
Students:	Four.
Mr. Jones:	Four. What is four times 180 degrees?

Jacquille:	Seven hundred twenty.
Mr. Jones:	Should be 720, right? How many degrees should there be in a five-sided figure? (Pause) Take the formula, the number of sides is five . . . subtract two and multiply by 180 degrees.
Mike:	Five hundred ninety?
Mr. Jones:	Five hundred forty degrees. All five-sided figures contain 540 degrees.

What is typical about the preceding segment is that the teacher stated the formula for the sum of the angles in a polygon and asked students to practice using the formula.

Reviewing Procedures and Definitions

After using the formula to calculate the sum of the interior angles in a triangle, Mr. Jones makes several announcements about upcoming activities and future quizzes and tests. He then conducts a quick oral review with the class on the meaning of such terms as complementary, supplementary, obtuse angle, and acute angle. A few minutes remain and Mr. Jones tells the students to use the time "to finish up any of this and ask me questions." The lesson ends with a bell, 48 minutes after it began. It is a bit unusual that no homework is assigned, but the length of the lesson is typical, just short of the U.S. average.

A JAPANESE LESSON

Reviewing the Previous Lesson

The bell rings and a student monitor asks all students to stand and bow. After the customary exchange of bows between the students and the teacher, the students sit down and engage in a bit of joking with Mr. Yoshida. He begins the lesson by reminding the students about the previous lesson. He asks "Do you remember what we did last period?" A student answers "We did mathematics." After more probing, a student replies that they obtained the "area of triangles which are [between] parallel lines."

"That's right," answers Mr. Yoshida, and he demonstrates the principle derived during the previous class. In a typical fashion the teacher underscores the importance of the principle—the equal areas of triangles with equivalent bases and heights. If the lesson proceeds as expected, this will set the stage for presenting the problem for the day, a problem in which the established principle will play an important role.

Presenting the Problem for the Day

"Prepare just your notebooks. We won't need your textbooks," says the teacher, drawing the following diagram on the board:

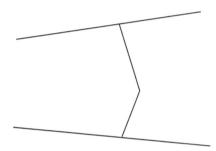

He explains that the land on one side of the bent line is Eda's land, while the land on the other side of the line is Azusa's land. While continuing to banter with the students, he says that the problem for the day is to draw a straight line replacing the bent line so that Eda and Azusa both end up with the same amount of land. After explaining some of the features of the problem, the teacher says, "Please try thinking about . . . methods of changing this shape without changing the area. Okay? Then everybody . . . let's try thinking about it. . . . Please think about it individually for three minutes. Okay, begin."

Working on the Problem Individually

For several minutes the students work individually on constructing a solution to the problem. Mr. Yoshida circulates around the room, answering questions and giving hints. A typical exchange:

Mr. Yoshida: You made that straight? Is it the same? Definitely?
Student: It's approximately.
Mr. Yoshida: If it's approximate, wouldn't they fight over it? . . .
Student: I can't solve it.
Mr. Yoshida: First of all, draw a figure. . . . Is there a method that uses the area of the triangles?

Working on the Problem in Groups

After working with the individual students for a few minutes, the teacher announces, "Okay, since the three minutes are up, people who have come up with an idea can check it with Teacher Hayakawa [a student teacher in the classroom], and people who want to discuss it with their friends discuss it with your friends. And for now I have placed some hint cards up here so people who want to refer to this can do so."

To this point the lesson has unfolded in typical fashion. The problem for the day has been presented by the teacher but only after students reviewed material that would allow them to begin solving it; students have worked individually for a time as the teacher moved around the room, observing their progress, giving hints, and taking notes. Now students shift to small groups to share what they have found and to continue trying to solve the problem. This is a challenging problem, and some students struggle to work out a solution.

One typical aspect of this lesson is that the students, rather than the teacher, are doing much of the mathematical work. Often, students have just learned procedures they can use to begin solving the new problems, and the teacher selects the problems and designs the lesson so that these new procedures are likely to be used.

Students Demonstrate Solutions

After some time Mr. Yoshida announces, "It's time, huh? Fifteen minutes." He then asks for a student to come to the board and demonstrate a solution. As the student diagrams a possible solution on the board, other students call out questions and suggestions. When the first student cannot arrive at a solution, the teacher asks a second student to come up and try. When that student also has trouble, the

SAMPLE EIGHTH-GRADE MATHEMATICS LESSONS
IN THE UNITED STATES AND JAPAN (CONTINUED)

teacher intervenes: "Then I'll draw it for you so, okay?" After considerable help from other students and the teacher, the class together arrives at a solution. "Okay, then applause. Wonderful."

Teacher Summarizes Solution and Presents Another Problem

The teacher then announces that since it is hard to see the solution he will make it clearer. He summarizes the students' method of solving the problems and polls the other students about which method they used.

He then presents another problem. "Without changing the area [of a quadrilateral drawn on the board], please try making it into a triangle. Okay, then, . . . please think three minutes and try doing it your own way."

Student: Teacher, can we open our textbooks yet?
Mr. Yoshida: The textbooks? First try thinking about it by yourselves, okay? You know that it was in the textbook, huh? [You're] sharp.

The process of working on the problem individually, in small groups, and with the teacher begins again. After about another 20 minutes of work, the teacher summarizes the results for the whole class. He draws the figure on the board and works through a solution. Toward the end of the solution, the bell rings to end class 49 minutes after it has begun. Concluding quickly, the teacher gives as a homework assignment the problem of converting a pentagon into a triangle with the same area.

Mr. Yoshido: You worked very hard, amazingly hard. Okay? . . . Then let's say the farewell properly.

At which point the students rise, bow to their teacher, and leave the room.

CHAPTER FIVE

What Does TIMSS Say About School Support Systems?

Just as curriculum and instruction affect student performance, the broader culture of a school and a society matters as well. Aspects of this culture include the preparation and support of teachers; attitudes toward the profession of teaching; the attitudes of teachers, students, and parents toward learning; and the lives of teachers and students, both inside and outside school. The TIMSS achievement tests, questionnaires, and case studies of the educational systems in Japan, Germany, and the United States all make the same point: these elements of the broader educational system and society can have an important influence on what students learn.

Many aspects of this broader culture are outside the control of teachers, school leaders, and policymakers. Nevertheless, the results of TIMSS point to differences among countries in school cultures that can be altered. These results suggest that school cultures are not given but are created and re-created by the decisions that teachers, administrators, students, and others make about how to organize teaching and learning.

As with the curriculum and instructional practices, the national standards in mathematics and science emphasize the importance of school support systems embedded in the broader culture. The science standards have separate sets of standards for science education systems and for the professional development of science teachers, which are both key elements of school support systems. Similarly, the volume *Professional Standards for Teaching Mathematics* (National Council of Teachers of Mathematics, 1991, p. 2) is based on two premises: "(1) Teachers are key figures in changing the ways in which mathematics is taught and learned in schools. (2) Such changes require that teachers have long-term support and adequate resources."

This chapter does not present particular aspects of the school culture as either good or bad. Rather, it describes a range of options across various dimensions of this culture. The aim is to bring these options to the attention of those responsible for making systemic informed attempts to improve school systems and academic achievement.

This chapter also is selective in its examination of school support systems, examining four particularly important influences on teaching and learning. The first section looks at time—primarily the structuring of teachers' time on a day-to-day level and its impact on collegiality among teachers. The second section examines teacher learning, including preservice preparation, new teachers' experiences, and ongoing professional development. The third section considers cultural influences on teaching, both at the school level and more broadly. The fourth section focuses on students' attitudes toward mathematics and science.

TEACHERS' TIME

For teachers across all countries, time is both a resource and a constraint. Through the TIMSS questionnaires, teachers outlined how they spend their time during the school week. The case studies of the educational systems in the United States, Germany, and Japan flesh out the picture of teachers' uses of time. While TIMSS did not draw conclusions about the uses of time in U.S. schools, the study demonstrates significant differences among countries that may bear closely on student achievement.

Time Pressures

The nature of teachers' work differs from country to country and among schools, but teachers everywhere say they are very busy.

According to questionnaire responses, teachers routinely spend time outside the formal school day to prepare and grade tests, read and grade student work, plan lessons, meet with students and parents, engage in professional development or reading, keep records, and complete administrative tasks. Fourth-grade teachers in the United States, for example, spent an average of 2.2 hours each week outside the formal school day preparing or grading tests, as well as 2.5 hours planning lessons. Similarly, each week on average their Japanese counterparts spent 2.4 hours on tests and 2.7 hours on lesson plans outside the school day.

QUESTIONS RELATED TO TEACHERS' TIME

• How does the daily schedule encourage or discourage collaboration among teachers?
• What opportunities are provided during the workday and over the course of the year for teachers to engage in professional development, planning, and collaboration?
• What are the trade-offs to providing teachers more time for professional development, planning, and collaboration—for example, would average class size grow, or would teachers need to do more of their planning outside school?

Recordkeeping and administrative tasks also took the U.S. teachers more than 3.5 hours each week and their Japanese peers just over 4 hours outside school (Martin et al., 1997, p. 137).

The TIMSS case studies reveal sharp contrasts among Germany, Japan, and the United States in the organization of school time, both daily and yearly (Table 5-1). Of the three, Japanese teachers have the longest official workday (8 to 9 hours, despite a slightly later average start time each day) and the longest work year (240 days). U.S. teachers put in longer official days than their German counterparts (7 to 8 hours in the United States and 5 to 5.5 hours in Germany) but have comparable work years (180 and 184 days, respectively).

Teachers also spend their time in school in somewhat different ways. Japanese teachers fulfill a broader range of in-school responsibilities than do German and U.S. teachers. For example, not only do they take turns supervising the playground, they also supervise lunch in their homerooms and the cleaning of a portion of the school each day (Stevenson and Nerison-Low, 1997, pp. 127-133).

Time to Collaborate

One of the most significant distinctions between Japanese and U.S. teachers' days is how much time they have to collaborate with colleagues (Tables 5-2a and 5-2b). Compared with Japanese teachers as a whole, U.S. teachers across all grade levels spend more of their assigned time in direct instruction and less in settings that allow for professional development, planning, and collaboration. As noted above, Japanese teachers also spend more time at school over the course of the day, which offers additional opportunities for collaboration. In addition, Japanese teachers often have the opportunity to observe each other's classes throughout the day (Kinney, 1998, pp. 223-227).

In Japan, teachers' time is structured in ways that enable collaboration. For example, in Japan, even brief breaks between classes become occasions for conversation. Instead of the 5 minutes between classes allowed in many U.S. schools, in Japan there might be 10- and sometimes 15-minute breaks between classes (Kinney, 1998, p. 225).

For the Japanese teachers observed in the case study, the boundaries between personal life and professional time often were not clear (Kinney, 1998, pp. 190-194). Many were heavily involved in school life not only in formal ways but also through informal study groups and other networks that strengthened their professional ties. While some Japanese teachers had

TABLE 5-1 Typical Features of a Teacher's Schedule in Japan, Germany, and the United States

	Japan	Germany	United States
School days per year (approximate)	240	184	180
Begin school day	8:00 a.m.	7:30 a.m.	7:30 a.m.
Classes end	3:30 p.m.	12:00 or 1:30 p.m.	2:45 p.m.
End of day at school	4:00 p.m. or later	12:30 to 1:30 p.m.	4:00 p.m. or later
Do schoolwork at home	Yes	Yes	Yes
Staff meetings			
Daily	Yes	—	—
Weekly	Yes	—	Varies
Monthly	Yes	Yes	Yes
Supervise			
Lunch	Daily in homeroom	—	Rotating
Playground	Rotating	Rotating	Rotating
Opportunity for collegial interaction			
Teachers' workroom	Yes	Yes	No
Lounge and hallways	Yes	Yes	Yes

Source: Stevenson and Nerison-Low, 1997, pp. 127-128.

family obligations that bounded their work day, for many, teaching, study, research, travel, and hobbies blended together and reinforced each other.

In contrast to Japan, Germany structures school time in ways that tend to isolate teachers from one another (Stevenson and Nerison-Low, 1997, pp. 131-132). Schedules in Germany require that the vast majority of teachers spend only the morning at school. Teachers normally go home soon after the students at midday, and they are expected to accomplish much of their planning and professional development outside the school day. In addition, with 23 to 27 periods per week in those half-day sessions, the schedule is packed, leaving teachers little time for the exchanges that punctuate Japanese teachers' days. While many Japanese teachers

build lesson planning, grading, and other school-related work into their time in the building, German teachers typically reported doing their out-of-class work at home.

TEACHER LEARNING

Preservice teacher education and later professional development are important factors contributing to the learning environment of students. Countries vary markedly in how they balance preservice and in-service education, where they locate professional development opportunities, whose expertise they consider most important to professional development, and the ways in which teacher learning unfolds, both formally and informally.

TABLE 5-2a Reports from Teachers Responsible for Teaching Science at the Fourth-Grade Level on How Often They Meet with Other Teachers to Discuss and Plan Curriculum or Teaching Approaches

Country	% of Students Taught by Teachers Who Meet with Their Colleagues			
	Never or Once/ Twice a Year	Monthly or Every Other Month	Once, Twice, or Three Times a Week	Almost Every Day
Australia	7	32	51	10
Austria	19	23	36	22
Canada	33	34	27	6
Cyprus	13	13	64	11
Czech Republic	3	13	31	52
England	4	12	75	13
Greece	32	26	26	16
Hong Kong	—	—	—	—
Hungary	2	13	45	41
Iceland	16	13	69	1
Iran, Islamic Republic	4	26	54	16
Ireland	46	42	7	5
Israel	10	42	41	7
Japan	5	14	61	20
Korea	17	24	41	18
Kuwait	7	1	75	17
Latvia (LSS)	14	28	32	26
Netherlands	36	33	29	2
New Zealand	10	17	60	13
Norway	4	7	82	7
Portugal	10	62	17	11
Scotland	9	37	40	14
Singapore	11	64	21	4
Slovenia	4	33	31	32
Thailand	62	23	13	1
United States	19	21	49	11

Source: Martin et al., 1997, p. 139.

Note: In most of the TIMSS countries, primary school classes are taught by a single teacher who is responsible for teaching all subjects in the curriculum. However, in a minority of countries, primary school students have different teachers for mathematics and science. In both Tables 5-2a and 5-2b, countries shown in italics did not satisfy one or more guidelines for sample participation rates, age/gender specifications, or classroom sampling procedures. A dash indicates that data are not available.

Teacher Preparation

The length of teacher training varies widely from one country to another. For population 1 and 2 teachers, required training in different countries ranges from only two years of postsecondary schooling to as many as six years (Martin et al., 1997, p. 129). Some countries require university preparation, others prescribe preparation in a teacher training institution,

TABLE 5-2b Reports from Mathematics Teachers at the Eighth-Grade Level on How Often They Meet with Other Teachers in Their Subject Area to Discuss and Plan Curriculum or Teaching

| Country | % of Students Taught by Teachers Who Meet with Their Colleagues | | | |
	Never or Once/ Twice a Year	Monthly or Every Other Month	Once, Twice, or Three Times a Week	Almost Every Day
Australia	10	50	30	9
Austria	20	37	36	6
Belgium (Fl)	48	28	21	3
Belgium (Fr)	22	34	38	7
Canada	38	25	31	6
Colombia	24	30	42	4
Cyprus	4	6	67	22
Czech Republic	22	23	34	20
Denmark	—	—	—	—
England	8	41	51	0
France	45	22	29	4
Germany	32	31	22	15
Greece	43	26	26	6
Hong Kong	33	48	19	0
Hungary	9	16	39	35
Iceland	42	29	29	0
Iran, Islamic Republic	18	37	34	11
Ireland	59	25	14	2
Israel	25	34	37	4
Japan	24	29	46	1
Korea	22	26	37	15
Kuwait	10	2	66	22
Latvia (LSS)	28	46	16	10
Lithuania	25	36	24	14
Netherlands	13	65	21	2
New Zealand	6	45	43	6
Norway	7	20	65	8
Portugal	8	69	18	5
Romania	12	58	14	16
Russian Federation	12	57	20	11
Scotland	7	12	74	8
Singapore	25	61	21	3
Slovak Republic	4	23	35	39
Slovenia	5	53	18	24
Spain	17	48	32	2
Sweden	9	19	46	26
Switzerland	36	32	30	2
Thailand	53	17	23	6
United States	37	31	26	6

Source: Beaton et al., 1996a, p.142.

**QUESTIONS RELATED TO TEACHER PREPARATION AND
TEACHER DEVELOPMENT**

• What is the balance of subject matter courses, pedagogical and methods courses, and practice teaching in the preservice education of prospective teachers? What does this balance imply about the way teaching is viewed as a profession?
• How is the induction of new teachers organized programmatically? Who and what are involved and to what end?
• What is the range of activities and content of staff development for teachers? How are these linked with curricular and instructional goals?
• How is professional development organized across the career of a teacher? What kinds of opportunities exist for what kinds of learning? What features support this?

and some require both. Most countries require a teaching practicum, and many require an examination or evaluation for certification (Mullis et al., 1997, p. 144; Beaton et al., 1996a, p. 132).

In the United States teacher preparation tends to be relatively extended compared with the teacher education required internationally, and it takes place in a variety of programs. Candidates learn to teach in university programs (typically a two-year liberal arts foundation followed by two years of professional preparation), postbaccalaureate and five-year programs, and alternative certification routes

(Stevenson and Nerison-Low, 1997, p. 121). Education courses make up a greater share of the coursework of those studying to teach elementary school than of those preparing to teach secondary school: 50 of 125 credits, on average, for future elementary teachers and 26 of 125 for secondary teachers. Student teaching experiences in the United States range from 6 to 18 weeks and have no uniform length or shape. While U.S. teachers stress the importance of student teaching to their learning, they often criticize the quality of supervision they receive.

Germany puts future teachers through a longer period of formal preparation than the

TABLE 5-3 Comparison of Teacher Training Requirements

Japan	Germany	United States
• Four years at a teachers' college or university	• Four to five years at a university	• Four years at a college or university
• Three to four weeks of practice teaching	• Two years of practice teaching	• One semester of practice teaching
• Prefectural certification exam	• First state exam	• State certification exam
• New teachers receive one year of in-school training under mentor and supplemental training in resource centers	• Second state exam	• Certification may be contingent on evaluation of first year of classroom work

Source: Stevenson and Nerison-Low, 1997, p. 116.

United States does (Table 5-3). Certification requirements depend in part on the level of school at which one will teach, but the typical pattern is four or five years of university preparation followed by two years of paid student teaching. Students pursuing certification to teach in one of Germany's academically selective high schools prepare in two subject areas and take extra courses in these areas, while those bound for academically less intense schools take more courses in general education (Milotich, 1996, p. 315). In Germany, university preparation is only the beginning of formal training. Preservice teachers take two certification examinations, one following university coursework and a second after the two years of student teaching. The first exam includes a written thesis in one's subject area or in education, written and oral examinations, and sometimes a practical exam (Milotich, 1996, p. 315). As many as two-thirds of students who begin university teacher preparation change career goals before reaching the first examination; among those who do take the first examination, "quite a few" never embark on student teaching (Milotich, 1996, p. 318). Student teaching, a phased experience, combines seminar study, classroom observation, assisted teaching, independent teaching, and preparation for the second state examination. Students work with mentor teachers in their subject areas as well as with seminar instructors who are themselves practicing teachers. The second state exam is judged by a committee of teachers, mentors, seminar instructors, and a representative of the state ministry of education. The committee weighs factors that include reports by mentor teachers; the

candidate's written thesis on lessons and units taught; and an oral examination on methodology, subject-related issues, or school laws and organization (Milotich, 1996, p. 321).

Germany's approach seems starkly different from U.S. approaches, but teachers in the two countries give surprisingly similar assessments of their preparation. German teachers said their university training was too theoretical, teacher preparation programs were fragmented, and inadequate guidance was offered. They considered student teaching very helpful but vulnerable to the weaknesses of mentors and seminar instructors. Many teachers said their mentors were ill prepared to help novices. Germany's mentor teachers receive no release time or compensation for their work.

In Japan, university graduates must take a highly competitive examination to qualify for a teaching position. Field experience for preservice teachers typically lasts a mere two to four weeks, but beginning teachers value it highly. The experience is seen less as an opportunity to put academic knowledge into practice than as a chance for learning the patterns of interaction that exist between teachers and pupils. While the Japanese preservice system seems to offer beginners little sustained support for learning their profession, the Japanese approach views preservice preparation as only a small beginning in a career launched and marked by mentoring relationships.

Professional Development for New Teachers

Professional development of teachers is as different among countries as teacher preparation. The case studies portray sharply different images of what professional development comprises, where and when it occurs, and the assumptions that underlie it. Not only do Germany, Japan, and the United States structure professional development opportunities differently, but differences in practice—how teachers experience professional development—exceed the differences in policy.

The United States appears to offer a less formal or coherent system of professional development than do Germany and Japan. Beginning teachers are expected immediately to take on the same duties and schedules as their more experienced peers, often without formal assistance. Although mentoring of first-year teachers is on the rise as official policy, there is no consistent approach to it. Communities vary greatly in such factors as the preparation and support given mentors and expectations for collaboration between mentors and novices.

Germany and Japan have more formal systems of induction to teaching. Just as Germany requires all new teachers to participate in a two-year, field-based student teaching experience, Japan assigns a mentor and requires additional study for first-year teachers. The German and Japanese approaches represent national policies that support the new teacher's transition from university preparation to work in schools. The German and Japanese approaches differ greatly from each other, however.

Germany's program is clearly a student teaching experience. While participants are paid (albeit less than licensed teachers), hired by districts, and work in schools, their experience—both the classroom experience and the associated seminar study and examination

preparation—is preparation, almost always for a position not in the school in which they are student teaching. While the teachers interviewed stressed the importance of the experience to their learning, they spoke less about the value of learning from other teachers and more about the importance of being grounded in practice (Milotich, 1996, p. 320).

Japan in the past decade has mandated an intensive mentoring and training program for all teachers in their first year on the job, a system reflecting the culture's widespread assumption that elders should guide novices. New teachers in their first year have at least 60 days of closely mentored teaching and 30 days of further training at resource centers run by local and prefectural boards of education. To allow for these activities, their teaching load is reduced (U.S. Department of Education, 1996, p. 51). Junior high and high school novices teach about 10 hours a week and go to the resource center one day each week. Of the 90 days of training provided to the newest teachers, 60 occur within the school (Kinney, 1998, p. 204). In its interweaving of practice and study and its practice of learning from colleagues, Japan's orientation to teacher learning seems consistent with the country's norms of professional development in many other fields.

Professional Development Over the Career

Japan displays a systematic orientation to lifelong learning, in contrast to the more ad hoc approaches taken by Germany and the United States to the professional development of experienced teachers.

Japanese teachers rotate among schools every six years, often changing grades as well.

This norm builds in new challenges for teachers, creates career cycles unlike those abroad, and constructs school cultures different from the relative stability that prevails in Germany and the United States. While remaining in a single school might be more comfortable, teachers believe it produces less growth. Similarly, Japanese teachers believe that teaching students of different ages enables them to understand children better (Kinney, 1998, pp. 209-211).

In addition, Japanese teachers in some areas engage in mandatory professional development away from their school in their sixth, tenth, and twentieth years. Reflecting on these experiences in the case study interviews, seasoned teachers suggested that the "content of the training was not always as important as the chance to mingle with peers and reflect upon one's job" (Kinney, 1998, p. 207).

Professional enhancement opportunities are quite varied in Japan. They range from formal training at local resource centers to voluntary mentoring and peer observation to lively teacher-organized informal study and action-research groups—a mode of professional development that teachers value highly. The case study found, in fact, that "most teachers voluntarily participate in teacher-run subject study groups that meet in the evening" (Kinney, 1998, p. 208) to examine videotapes of practice, study new curricula, discuss textbooks, and so on. Some communities offer professional development fellowships or sabbaticals to support teacher research in an "in-country exchange study," with teachers released for a few weeks from their school to travel to study in a place they choose. A range

of national, regional, and local study grants send teachers traveling domestically and abroad (Kinney, 1998, p. 205). All these practices reflect the assumption that teachers need broad knowledge.

Interestingly, German teachers tended to say that a critical part of success in teaching is "an openness and willingness to learn" (Milotich, 1996, p. 310). Yet they did not share Japanese teachers' assumption about the centrality of peers to one's learning. Instead, in Germany, "some teachers, in talking about how such learning occurred, referred to journals that they read regularly. Science teachers, in particular, talked about the importance of keeping current with the subject matter" (Milotich, 1996, p. 310).

The case study report on Germany concludes that "teachers at all stages of their careers lack formal support" (Milotich, 1996, p. 326). There are many "state-sponsored institutions and academies offering continuing-education courses for experienced teachers" (Milotich, 1996, p. 329). In addition, schools bring in "experts" to address issues identified as problems in the school. Continuing education, however, is not required in most states, and participation seems to be highest among less experienced teachers.

U.S. schools and school districts offer a range of staff development programs, but these tend to be short-term, vary widely in focus, and often appear to teachers as a menu of unrelated opportunities for stimulation or growth. Districts vary in the degree to which they try to induce teachers to take advantage of these opportunities. Although some districts engage in more systematic efforts at sustained professional development, short-term workshops remain the dominant format. Teachers in the case study were "only peripherally aware" of approaches to professional development that grow out of practice and allow teachers "to study and improve their own practice" (Lubeck, 1996, p. 259).

While the case studies suggest generalizations, it would be a mistake to regard cultural differences as rigid determinants of teachers' experiences. These experiences are dynamic, not fixed. Japan's recent mandates for formal teacher support, Germany's newest approaches to teacher preparation, and emerging U.S. policies on mentoring all demonstrate that the context of professional development is changing and that teachers of different ages have had different experiences as approaches to professional development have evolved.

CULTURAL INFLUENCES ON TEACHING

Arrangements of teachers' time and approaches to teacher learning contribute greatly to school culture, but culture encompasses more subtle factors as well. Without labeling these factors as either good or bad, it is useful to look at the range of choices that school personnel make in various dimensions of schooling. Through these choices, school personnel situate their schools at particular points along continuums of cultural variables. This section examines two such continuums illuminated by TIMSS. The first describes how teachers work—the continuum from community to autonomy—while the second describes their status—the continuum from professional to skilled worker.

Underlying these continua are striking international similarities in how teachers view their work. The salient picture that emerges from the case studies is of people who are dedicated to teaching but who, especially in the United States, are enduring frustrations and even fatigue in their professional lives. In other countries the frequency and intensity of these problems tend to be less serious, but they are equally disturbing to the teachers involved. Many teachers believe the demands they face have increased in recent years, and high school teachers "find the heightened emphasis on [high-stakes] examinations to be among the

---

QUESTIONS RELATED TO CULTURAL INFLUENCES ON TEACHING

- What supports a sense of community among teachers? What inhibits it? What supports autonomy among teachers, and what inhibits it?
- How could the relative emphasis between teacher autonomy and community be changed?
- How do arrangements of space and time contribute to the culture of teaching? How do other policies affect this culture?
- What kinds of collegiality among teachers are encouraged and how?
- In what ways are teachers treated as professionals or as skilled workers? How could these relative emphases be changed?

most troublesome demands currently made of teachers in all three countries" (Stevenson and Nerison-Low, 1997, p. 140).

The Continuum from Community to Autonomy

The challenge of school leadership is to maximize the impact of individual strengths and the collective capacity of the instructional staff. How to do both at once is a challenge every school faces, and TIMSS describes very different approaches and decisions that schools make in this regard.

Japanese teachers have desks in a shared teachers' room, and teachers with common assignments may have neighboring desks in order to exchange ideas, plan together easily, and more naturally and frequently interact (Kinney, 1998, pp. 220-225). This shared office space opens some part of teachers' work to others' view, which can, at different times, be either enabling or constraining.

This arrangement contrasts with teachers' lounges and staff rooms, the common situation in the United States and Germany, where there is no structure of desks or space that supports interactions around teaching. Some U.S. and German schools provide spaces where teachers can and do come together meaningfully, but these are the exceptions, the case studies indicate. German teachers have little time for interaction during the day, and most U.S. teachers have very limited time and also say they are drawn to work in their own class-rooms. There are important exceptions to these general observations, however. In one U.S. case study school, teachers did meet every day, and the schedule was arranged to maximize teacher collaboration.

Authentic collegiality depends not only on policies and space but also on assumptions about teaching and the work of teachers. This is suggested in one way by a German teacher who said, "I do not want to open myself to other teachers because they could use my openness to talk about me in a bad way" (Milotich, 1996, p. 352). In another way it is suggested by the expectations for teachers in Japan. There, teachers are encouraged to engage with one another as colleagues and resources. In Germany, Japan, and the United States alike, schools in which teachers were able to see themselves as having a common pur-pose—such as a German school devoted to educating immigrant children—were best able to support this kind of collaborative culture (Milotich, 1996, p. 353).

It is important to remember, however, that the TIMSS data on teacher collegiality are not clear cut. Teachers in some high-achieving countries claim to meet very frequently (81 percent of Japanese students at the fourth-grade level are taught by teachers who meet at least once each week), while others report infrequent meetings (in Hong Kong, another high achiever, 81 percent of students in the upper grade of population 2 are taught by teachers who report meeting no more than once a month; see Tables 5-2a and 5-2b earlier in this chapter).

The Continuum from Professionals to Skilled Workers

Teachers are members of a professional community that, by definition, assumes lifelong learning as a goal. However, they also are hired as skilled workers who are presumed to be prepared and ready to teach.

Schools vary in how they balance these dual assumptions. As described in previous sections, some schools treat teachers as members of a profession through the ways in which they hire them, organize their time, afford teachers control of certain aspects of their work and time, provide opportunities for continued learning, and facilitate collegial relationships among educators. Other schools construct cultures that treat teachers only as skilled workers. They provide the setting for the work of instruction but make few provisions for other dimensions of practice.

Although Japanese teachers described their profession as reasonably well respected, they worried about their situation. "Despite relatively high levels of support, training and respect, teachers were quick to wish for even more support, criticize training as too systematic, [and] bemoan the fact that sufficient training does not occur in every school and that the status of teachers cannot be taken for granted" (Kinney, 1998, p. 189). Japanese teachers said their profession is respected but not as much as it was in the past.

German teachers, by contrast, complained that they were stigmatized as part-time workers. In the eye of the general public, teachers have long vacations (12 weeks in all) and afternoons off. Although German teachers structure a large portion of their work time themselves, they emphasized that, while at school, they work almost nonstop in a fast-paced, high-stress environment. They said most people do not realize how much time they spend at home preparing for classes and grading exams. "They expressed frustration with the expectations placed on teachers and disappointment with what they perceive as declining respect for their profession" (Milotich, 1996, pp. 337-338).

In addition, the material and symbolic benefits that accrue to teachers help to situate them on a continuum from professional to skilled worker. For example, competition for entry into the profession is an important measure of how teaching is viewed (Table 5-4). In Germany and Japan, competition is high, as evidenced by the rigor of teacher preparation and entrance examinations. Researchers on the Japanese TIMSS case study believed this competition bolstered the status of teaching, which they described as "fairly well respected" (Kinney, 1998, p. 186). Competitiveness varies by field, however. In the humanities there are about 30 applicants for each position, while rates are closer to 10 to 1 in mathematics and science teaching—a phenomenon probably due to self-selection. One teacher explained that competition to become a mathematics teacher is less fierce than to become a teacher of other subjects simply because the mathematics coursework is so demanding: "Those who are just so-so at math won't make it" (Kinney, 1998, p. 203).

In economic terms, teaching in Japan compares favorably with other occupations (Kinney, 1998, p. 188). Because of the importance accorded teaching at all levels of education, the salaries of public school teachers are not far below those of university professors (Stevenson and Nerison-Low, 1997, p. 124). Salaries are based on length of service to the school district. As in many professions in Japan, the basic year-long salary for teachers is supplemented by bonuses equivalent to up to

TABLE 5-4 Factors Indicating Desirability of Teaching Profession

	Japan	Germany	United States
Competing to enter teaching profession	High	High	Varies by location
Salary, bonus, benefits	Above average	Above average	Varies by location
Occupational status	Above average	Civil servant: varies by type of school	Average to low

Source: Stevenson and Nerison-Low, 1997, p. 123.

five month's salary and allowances for certain personal and professional expenses.

In contrast, U.S. teachers earn less on average than professionals in other fields with comparable years of university and graduate education. According to the 1997 survey and analysis of salary trends conducted by the American Federation of Teachers (available at http://www.aft.org/research/salary/home.htm), the 1996-97 average teacher salary was $38,436. Salaries in other white-collar occupations tended to be higher, from 74 percent more for attorneys to 10 percent more for accountants. This pay differential has contributed to a shortage of mathematics and science teachers in some parts of the country, which has forced schools to rely on teaching out of field and teachers who have gone through alternative certification tracks.

German teachers are compensated according to a national civil service pay scale (Milotich, 1996, p. 340). Their salaries—ranging from about $35,000 to $40,000—depend on the type of school or level at which they teach, as well as their years of service, marital status, and family size.

Employment benefits also differ among Germany, Japan, and the United States (Table 5-5). All teachers in the three countries receive medical, retirement, and vacation benefits, although the specifics vary. In addition, teachers in Japan are "eligible as civil servants for extra monetary allowances for dependents, financial adjustments (such as cost of living), housing, transportation, assignments to outlying areas, administrative positions, periodic costs (such as those incurred when traveling with sports teams), and diligent service" (Kinney, 1998, p. 188). Japanese national and local education authorities also offer teachers travel and study options.

The German case study suggests that job security is one benefit associated with teaching in that country. As civil servants, German teachers cannot be laid off.

STUDENT ATTITUDES

Internationally, students tend to share positive attitudes toward math and science. Most U.S. fourth and eighth graders report that they like both mathematics and science, though more fourth graders liked these subjects than eighth graders. However, the decline in

TABLE 5-5 Teachers' Compensation Packages

Japan	Germany	United States
National pay scale	Civil servant pay scale in former West German states; separate pay scale for teachers in former East German states	District pay scales
Salary based on level of school, type of position, level of responsibility, years of teaching experience	Civil servant pay scale based on years of education required; pay increases with years of service	Determined by degree attained, years of teaching experience, and location Merit-based raises adopted in some districts
Bonuses twice a year	Christmas bonus	None
Allowance for family composition, remote area, special services, vocational education, end of year, and extreme climate	Allowance for households, based on marital status and family size, usually 30 to 35% of base salary	None
Benefits: medical, retirement, vacation, housing, investment plan, low-interest loans	Benefits: medical, retirement, vacation, dental	Benefits: medical, retirement, vacation, dental, life insurance

Source: Stevenson and Nerison-Low, 1997, p. 115.

QUESTIONS RELATED TO STUDENT ATTITUDES

- Why do students think that it is or is not important to achieve high levels of understanding in mathematics and science?
- How is student performance in these subjects related to their beliefs about them?

---

affection for mathematics and science from fourth to eighth grade in the United States is typical internationally (U.S. Department of Education, 1997b, p. 50).

Where differences in student attitudes emerge among countries, TIMSS findings have interesting implications for student achievement. Most notably, while most students in most countries think they do well in mathematics and science, students in some of the highest-performing countries recorded markedly lower perceptions of their own performance. For example, in almost all TIMSS countries, most population 2 students said they did well in mathematics, but three of the four countries in which this was not true—Hong Kong, Japan, and Korea—were among the highest-performing countries (Beaton et al., 1996a, p. 117). Similarly, in all countries except those three, most students said they did well in either integrated science or science as a whole, yet Japan and Korea were among the highest-performing countries in science (Beaton, 1996a, p. 111). These findings suggest that students in high-performing countries may work especially hard to meet perceived shortcomings.

Data from TIMSS indicate that U.S. students also believe that hard work is important in learning mathematics and science. Students expressed this belief at the same time, however, that they devoted relatively little out-of-class time to studying and more to job-related activities (National Research Council, 1998; Schmidt et al., 1999, pp. 109-110). For example, U.S. students in population 3 work significantly more than their peers internationally (Figure 5-1).

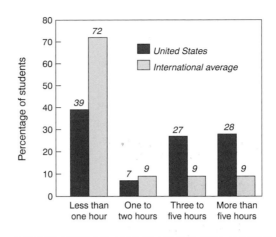

FIGURE 5-1 U.S. twelfth-grade students' reports on number of hours on a normal school day spent working at a paid job in comparison with the international average. Source: U.S. Department of Education, 1998, p. 68.

CHAPTER SIX

Frequently Asked Questions About TIMSS

TIMSS has produced a storehouse of information that will take many years to analyze thoroughly. It also has provided a snapshot of the educational systems in the United States and many other countries. As these systems change in future years, the results of TIMSS will provide a baseline against which improvements can be measured.

This report highlights many of the key findings from TIMSS and relates those findings to the implementation of standards-based education in the United States. The goal of this report is not to recommend specific courses of action or to define a research agenda that can address remaining questions. Instead, by offering information from TIMSS as an analytical tool, this report seeks to further local improvements in schools made by the many different individuals with a stake in U.S. education.

This final chapter offers a set of questions that are often asked about TIMSS along with brief responses to those questions.

What information was TIMSS designed to gather?

TIMSS gathered information in five different categories. It gave timed paper-and-pencil tests to more than half a million children in 41 different countries to test their understanding and skills in mathematics and science (a more limited number of students also participated in a performance assessment consisting of 12 hands-on tasks). It administered questionnaires to students, teachers, and administrators to gauge such factors as student attitudes toward mathematics and science, teacher backgrounds, and school policies and practices. It analyzed more than 1,000 textbooks and curriculum guides from participating countries to investigate curricular patterns. It videotaped a total of 231 representative eighth-grade mathematics classrooms in the United States, Germany, and Japan to analyze mathematics teaching in practice. And it conducted case studies of educational policies and practices in the same three countries.

Which groups of students were studied?

TIMSS assessed the achievement of students at three stages of their education. At the elementary school level, TIMSS administered achievement tests to students in the two adjacent grades containing the most 9 year olds (a group referred to as population 1, corresponding to grades three and four in the United States). At the lower secondary school level, students were studied in the two adjacent grades containing the most 13 year olds (population 2, or seventh and eighth grade in the United States). At the upper secondary

school level, TIMSS assessed the mathematical and scientific proficiency of students in their last year of secondary school (population 3, corresponding to U.S. high school seniors).

In a nutshell, how did U.S. students compare to their international peers on the student achievement assessments in mathematics and science?

The youngest U.S. students had the highest comparative achievement. In elementary school science and mathematics, U.S. students scored near the top of all students in science and among a band of countries scoring above the international average in mathematics. U.S. middle school students continued to exceed the international average in science but fell below it in mathematics. High school seniors in the United States were below the international average in general knowledge of both subjects and even further behind in separate tests of physics and advanced mathematics.

Another way to compare is to ask what percentage of each nation's students rank among the top 10 percent internationally. In elementary school mathematics, 9 percent of U.S. fourth graders would make that cut—almost a representative share but far fewer than in the strongest countries; 39 percent of the upper-grade population 1 students in Singapore are in the top 10 percent internationally. In elementary school science, 16 percent of U.S. fourth graders make the top 10 percent. In middle school, 13 percent of U.S. eighth graders are in the top echelon for science, and 5 percent are for mathematics—again, well behind top-ranked Singapore, which had 45 percent of its upper-grade students rank in the top 10 percent internationally in mathematics.

The pattern revealed by TIMSS has essentially held true in international comparisons over the past decade and a half—not stellar performance, not last, and stronger among younger students, especially in science. In fact, it is unlikely that U.S. students' standing has changed much over the past 30 years.

In what subjects or educational characteristics is the United States strongest relative to other nations? Where is it weakest?

U.S. strengths tend to match what is emphasized in U.S. curricula. U.S. elementary and middle school students do comparatively well in earth science, life science, and environmental issues and the nature of science. They do less well in physical science at this age, and performance in this area continued to fade in later years. By the final year of secondary school, U.S. scores in physics are among the lowest of the nations participating in TIMSS.

In mathematics, U.S. elementary and middle school students are comparatively strong in number sense and data representation and analysis, with the younger group also excelling in patterns, relations, functions, and geometry. U.S. students are weak in measurement at both grade levels, and from elementary school to middle school performance in geometry moves from above to below the international average.

One explanation suggested by TIMSS for U.S. students' slide in rank is that they are not challenged enough. Eighth-grade mathematics in the United States is covered in seventh grade in high-achieving countries, and U.S. math-

ematics teachers demand less sophisticated thinking than do teachers in Germany and Japan. As a result, U.S. students learn more slowly than is the norm abroad, making less progress from one grade to the next than students in most countries.

Did TIMSS compare all U.S. students with just the best students in other countries?

The designers of TIMSS sought to have all countries, as much as possible, test comparable groups of students. Drawing on critiques of past international comparisons, they established rigorous new procedures to make sure that students taking the tests were randomly selected to represent all students in their nations. An international committee scrutinized the selection process in each country for compliance with these procedures. When nations did not meet the standards—for example, because too many schools, teachers, or students declined to participate—these exceptions were noted to allow researchers to take them into account.

Even so, meeting the selection criteria did not necessarily disadvantage a country in the rankings. Countries that met the criteria for the fourth- and eighth-grade tests included Korea and Japan, which generally outperformed the United States, as well as the Czech Republic, Hong Kong, and Singapore, which performed well in many areas.

The concern that all U.S. students are being compared unfairly to elite students abroad runs deepest in regard to the last year of secondary school. The conventional wisdom is that in some other countries only the best students are still in school at that age. In fact, to the extent that biases can be identified in the population 3 samples, most of them should have favored the United States. For example, the United States has proportionally fewer 17 year olds enrolled than the average of other TIMSS countries with enrollment data. Since students who drop out presumably tend to be lower achievers, this phenomenon may enhance the relative rank of the United States.

It is true that most countries participating in the end-of-secondary school tests, including the United States, did not meet the selection criteria for representative samples. Nevertheless, important conclusions can be drawn from the results. The fact that some of the highest-achieving U.S. students had not taken equally advanced courses as their foreign peers is itself a point to consider. Furthermore, a particularly weak area of performance among seniors was in geometry, a curricular area that is emphasized in U.S. high schools.

Aren't students at the end of secondary school too varied in age, from one country to another, to compare them?

The U.S. students in population 3 were somewhat younger than the international average: 18.1 years old compared to an average of 18.7 among all 21 nations participating in this level of TIMSS achievement testing. The disparity was half as great for the subset of students who took the advanced science and mathematics tests: the average U.S. age was 18.0, while the average age among all nations participating in this special test was 18.4 years for physics and 18.3 years for mathematics.

In addition, age was not strictly correlated with performance. Australia and New Zealand did better than the United States on the mathematics and science general assessment, but their students were on average younger than those in the United States. The performance of Russian students was on a par with that of U.S. students despite being a year younger and having had a year less of formal schooling.

Several other factors also minimize the importance of the age differences among students in population 3. First, the TIMSS general tests for secondary school seniors are essentially literacy tests, not examinations on advanced knowledge. The mathematics topics were similar to topics covered by the seventh grade in most countries, and the science topics generally were covered by the ninth grade. High school seniors all should have been exposed to the material.

Finally, unlike the tests of the two younger populations, the test of high school seniors was not intended to compare students of the same age. Secondary school graduation is a turning point in all countries—the threshold of adulthood and of important choices among work and further study. International variation in the ages and knowledge levels at which adolescents cross that threshold is not only inevitable but interesting in and of itself.

Isn't TIMSS just a "horserace" that puts too much emphasis on test scores without revealing substantive insights into our educational system?

Some people may choose to focus selectively on the quantitative country scores derived from the TIMSS data, but TIMSS as a whole produced much more than just measures of student achievement. It yielded qualitative and quantitative information about the attitudes, lifestyles, teaching, and educational policies that contribute to academic strengths and weaknesses in each country. As such, the study is a tool for comparing educational policies and practices and finding the roots of relatively strong and weak performance.

At the same time, even the achievement test scores that prompt the "horserace" complaint are valuable because they demonstrate a shortfall between U.S. performance and that of the highest-achieving countries. Furthermore, TIMSS presented the country scores in a more statistically meaningful way than the typical newspaper summary, grouping countries in broad bands of achievement instead of making much of small differences between countries that are effectively on a par with each other.

Don't cultural differences among the TIMSS countries render test score comparisons meaningless?

Differences are what make TIMSS valuable and interesting. Cultural differences are an argument against simplistic interpretations of TIMSS, not an argument against TIMSS itself. Data from the student questionnaires illustrate why. For example, U.S. high school seniors study less, with more optimism, than do their peers in many countries. TIMSS does not say these cultural traits determine our standing internationally, but the data bring to light possible contributing factors and suggest questions for further research.

Educational goals and philosophies, social values, school safety, teachers' ideas about student ability, how students spend their time—countless factors that stem from culture affect student performance. One goal of TIMSS was therefore to identify and examine these differences.

Did TIMSS prove that the U.S. curriculum is "a mile wide and an inch deep"?

On the face of it, TIMSS data suggest that U.S. schools cover an exceptionally high number of topics every year at most levels relative to mathematics and science classes in other countries. This has led educators to ask: Is U.S. teaching more superficial? Would U.S. students do better with fewer topics covered in more depth?

U.S. science and mathematics textbooks do cover many more topics than is typical in other countries' books. Furthermore, the United States tends to repeat topics over more years than do other countries, at least in mathematics. The data sketch a picture of repeated exposure without time for mastery.

However, the overall picture is not necessarily black and white. For one thing, the number of topics covered is not necessarily a sign of bad teaching. A teacher who covers many topics may be spending a lot of time on a few topics while briefly touching on others. A teacher also may cover many topics to draw connections among different areas of the curriculum. Or a teacher who revisits topics may go deeper each time.

Other indicators, however, continue to point to problems in U.S. curricula. The videotapes of eighth-grade mathematics classes in three countries showed U.S. teachers presenting less sophisticated topics and evoking a lower level of student reasoning than their German and Japanese peers. Depth of coverage also may suffer from the fact that U.S. teachers changed topics more often than did teachers in Germany and Japan, and their lessons were more likely to be interrupted.

What did TIMSS discover about the conventional ways of teaching in different countries?

Teaching practices reflect particular instructional goals, beliefs about science and mathematics and how they are learned, and assumptions about what a normal lesson looks like. Lessons vary, obviously, but TIMSS suggests that each culture may have typical "scripts" for teaching mathematics and science.

As demonstrated in the videotapes and case studies, the typical U.S. script emphasizes incremental mastery of a sequence of skills. A frustrated student is a signal that previous material was not conveyed adequately. In Japan, in contrast, frustration can be normal and useful in a lesson. Students there may be asked to invent ways to solve a new problem, and their struggle sets the stage on which the teacher brings out new concepts and shows relationships among concepts and facts.

In each country a typical sequence of actions carries this script forward. In a U.S. middle school mathematics class, the teacher typically reviews previous material, often by checking homework; then demonstrates how to solve the day's new problems; has the students practice on their own; and, finally, corrects their practice problems. The equivalent teacher in Japan

reviews by lecturing or questioning the students, poses problems and has students work on them individually and perhaps in groups, leads a class discussion of how to solve the problems, and concludes by clarifying and summarizing the main concepts.

Germany is closer in practice to the United States than Japan. German and U.S. students do mathematics by following the teacher's lead. Japanese students do the same at times, but at other times their job is to think creatively about the subject. Open-ended questions and close-ended quizzing both have their place in Japan, but teachers in Germany and the United States do much more of the latter.

Consistent with the U.S. emphasis on skill, U.S. teachers give more time to review than in the highest-achieving countries. Most U.S. students received only 10 minutes of instruction on new material in a typical eighth-grade mathematics class, and a similar pattern seems to hold true for science. U.S. teachers also tend to vary lessons by changing topics, while Japanese teachers are more apt to stay on one topic but shift often from classwork to individual work to small-group work and back again. U.S. elementary and middle school teachers are unusual in giving students class time to begin their homework, and they give more quizzes than other teachers.

Did TIMSS find any one factor that causes higher student performance?

This is what everyone would love to find—a sure-fire prescription for improving education. TIMSS demonstrates that there isn't one. Education and learning involve countless variables, from teacher education and parental attitudes to class size and students' after-school jobs. The variables all affect learning, and no single one has been shown to be overwhelmingly influential.

Education is generally too complex to link causes and effects conclusively. TIMSS turned up many counterexamples for arguments attempting to ascribe achievement to particular variables. For instance, while many people believe that smaller class size is associated with higher achievement, classes in Korea, one of the top-performing countries, average more than 40 students.

The results of TIMSS also reiterate that some factors affecting achievement are not immediately within schools' control. For example, parents' education levels and the number of books in the home were related to student achievement.

References

American Association for the Advancement of Science. 1993. *Benchmarks for Science Literacy.* New York: Oxford University Press.

Baker, David P. 1997a. "Good News, Bad News, and International Comparisons: Comment on Bracey." *Educational Researcher*, 26(April):16-17.

Baker, David P. 1997b. "Surviving TIMSS." *Phi Delta Kappan*, (Dec.):295-300.

Beaton, Albert E., Ina V. S Mullis, Michael O. Martin, Eugenio J. Gonzalez, Dana L. Kelly, and Teresa A. Smith. 1996a. *Mathematics Achievement in the Middle School Years: IEA's Third International Mathematics and Science Study (TIMSS).* Chestnut Hill, Mass.: TIMSS International Study Center, Boston College.

Beaton, Albert E., Michael O. Martin, Ina V. S Mullis, Eugenio J. Gonzalez, Teresa A. Smith, and Dana L. Kelly. 1996b. *Science Achievement in the Middle School Years: IEA's Third International Mathematics and Science Study (TIMSS).* Chestnut Hill, Mass.: TIMSS International Study Center, Boston College.

Beatty, Alexander, ed. 1997. *Learning from TIMSS: Results of the Third International Mathematics and Science Study. Summary of a Symposium.* Washington, D.C.: National Academy Press.

Bracey, Gerald W. 1996. "International Comparisons and the Condition of American Education." *Educational Researcher,* 25(Jan.-Feb.):5-11.

Bracey, Gerald W. 1997. "On Comparing the Incomparable: A Response to Baker and Stedman." *Educational Researcher,* 26(April): 19-26.

Bracey, Gerald W. 1998. "Tinkering with TIMSS." *Phi Delta Kappan,* (Sept.):32-36.

Business Coalition for Education Reform. 1998. *The Formula for Success: A Business Leader's Guide to Supporting Math and Science Achievement.* Washington, D.C.: U.S. Department of Education.

Forgione, Pascal D., Jr. 1998. "Responses to Frequently Asked Questions About 12th-Grade TIMSS." *Phi Delta Kappan,* (June):769-772.

Harmon, M., T.A. Smith, M.O. Martin, D.L. Kelly, A.E. Beaton, I.V.S. Mullis, E.J. Gonzalez, and G. Orpwood. 1997. *Performance Assessment in IEA's Third International Mathematics and Science Study (TIMSS).* Chestnut Hill, Mass.: TIMSS International Study Center, Boston College.

Kinney, C. 1998. "Teachers and the Teaching Profession in Japan." Pp. 183-253 in *The Educational System in Japan: Case Study Findings.* Washington, D.C.: U.S. Department of Education.

Lapointe, A. E., J. M. Askew, and N. A. Mead. 1992. *Learning Science.* Princeton, N.J.: Educational Testing Service.

Lubeck, S. 1996. "Teachers and the Teaching Profession in the United States." Pp. 241-318 in the draft volume of *The Education System in the United States: Case Study Findings.* Ann Arbor: University of Michigan Center for Human Growth and Development.

Manaster, Alfred B. 1998. "Some Characteristics of Eighth Grade Mathematics Classes in the TIMSS Videotape Study." *The American Mathematical Monthly,* 105(Nov.):793-805.

Martin, Michael O., Ina V.S. Mullis, Albert E. Beaton, Eugenio J. Gonzalez, Teresa A. Smith, and Dana L. Kelly. 1997. *Science Achievement in the Primary School Years: IEA's Third International Mathematics and Science Study (TIMSS).* Chestnut Hill, Mass.: TIMSS International Study Center, Boston College.

McKnight, C. C., F. J. Crosswhite, J. A. Dossey, E. Kifer, J. O. Swafford, K. J. Travers, and T. J. Cooney. 1989. *The Underachieving Curriculum: Assessing U.S. School Mathematics from an International Perspective.* Champaign, Ill.: Stipes Publishing Co.

Milotich, U. 1996. "Teachers and the Teaching Profession in Germany." Pp. 295-379 in the draft volume of *The Education System in Germany: Case Study Findings.* Ann Arbor: University of Michigan Center for Human Growth and Development.

Mullis, Ina V. S., Michael O. Martin, Albert E. Beaton, Eugenio J. Gonzalez, Dana L. Kelly, and Teresa A. Smith. 1997. *Mathematics Achievement in the Primary School Years: IEA's Third International Mathematics and Science Study (TIMSS).* Chestnut Hill, Mass.: TIMSS International Study Center, Boston College.

Mullis, Ina V.S., Michael O. Martin, Albert E. Beaton, Eugenio J. Gonzalez, Dana L. Kelly, and Teresa A. Smith. 1998. *Mathematics and Science Achievement in the Final Year of Secondary School: IEA's Third International Mathematics and Science Study (TIMSS).* Chestnut Hill, Mass.: TIMSS International Study Center, Boston College.

National Council of Teachers of Mathematics. 1989. *Curriculum and Evaluation Standards for School Mathematics.* Reston, Va.: National Council of Teachers of Mathematics.

National Council of Teachers of Mathematics. 1991. *Professional Standards for Teaching Mathematics.* Reston, Va.: National Council of Teachers of Mathematics.

National Council of Teachers of Mathematics. 1998. *Principles and Standards for School Mathematics: Discussion Draft.* Reston, Va.: National Council of Teachers of Mathematics.

National Research Council. 1996. *National Science Education Standards.* Washington, D.C.: National Academy Press.

National Research Council. 1997. *What Have We Learned About Making Education Standards Internationally Competitive?* Washington, D.C.: National Academy Press.

National Research Council. 1998. *Protecting Youth at Work: Health, Safety, and Development of Working Children and Adolescents in the United States.* Washington, D.C.: National Academy Press.

National Research Council. 1999. *Designing Mathematics or Science Curriculum Programs: A Guide for Using Mathematics and Science Standards.* Washington, D.C.: National Academy Press.

Robitaille, David F., ed. 1997. *National Contexts for Mathematics and Science Education.* Vancouver, Canada: Pacific Educational Press.

Rotberg, Iris C. 1998. "Interpretation of International Test Score Comparisons." *Science,* 280(May 15):1030-1031.

Schmidt, William H., and Curtis C. McKnight. 1998. "What Can We Really Learn from TIMSS?" *Science,* 282(Dec. 4):1830-1831.

Schmidt, William H., Curtis C. McKnight, Gilbert A. Valverde, Richard T. Houang, and David E. Wiley. 1997a. *Many Visions, Many Aims: Volume 1: A Cross-National Investigation of Curricular Intentions in School Mathematics.* Boston: Kluwer Academic Publishers.

Schmidt, William H., Curtis C. McKnight, Gilbert A. Valverde, Richard T. Houang, and David E. Wiley. 1997b. *Many Visions, Many Aims: Volume 2: A Cross-National Exploration of Curricular Intentions in School Science.* Boston: Kluwer Academic Publishers.

Schmidt, William H., Curtis C. McKnight, and Senta A. Raizen. 1997c. *Splintered Vision: An Investigation of U.S. Science and Mathematics Education.* Boston: Kluwer Academic Publishers.

Schmidt, William H., et al. 1999. *Facing the Consequences: Using TIMSS for a Closer Look at U.S. Mathematics and Science Education.* Boston: Kluwer Academic Publishers.

Stedman, Lawrence C. 1997. "International Achievement Differences: An Assessment of a New Perspective." *Educational Researcher,* 26(April):4-15.

Stevenson, Harold W. 1998. "A Study of Three Cultures. Germany, Japan, and the United States—An Overview of the TIMSS Case Study Project." *Phi Delta Kappan,* (March):524-529.

Stevenson, Harold W., and Roberta Nerison-Low. 1997. *To Sum It Up: Case Studies of Education in Germany, Japan, and the United States.* Washington, D.C.: U.S. Government Printing Office.

Stigler, J. W., and James Hiebert. 1997. "Understanding and Improving Classroom Mathematics Instruction: An Overview of the TIMSS Video Study." *Phi Delta Kappan,* 79(Sept.):14-21.

Stigler, James W., and James Hiebert. 1999. *The Teaching Gap.* New York: Free Press.

Stigler, James W., Patrick Gonzales, Takako Kawanaka, Steffen Knoll, and Ana Serrano. 1999. *The TIMSS Videotape Classroom Study: Methods and Findings from an Exploratory Research Project on Eighth-Grade Mathematics Instruction in Germany, Japan, and the United States.* Washington, D.C.: U.S. Government Printing Office.

U.S. Department of Education. 1992. *International Mathematics and Science Assessments: What Have We Learned?* Washington, D.C.: U.S. Department of Education.

U.S. Department of Education. 1996. *Pursuing Excellence: A Study of U.S. Eighth-Grade Mathematics and Science Teaching, Learning, Curriculum, and Achievement in International Context.* Washington, D.C.: U.S. Government Printing Office.

U.S. Department of Education. 1997a. *Introduction to TIMSS.* Washington, D.C.: U.S. Department of Education.

U.S. Department of Education. 1997b. *Pursuing Excellence: A Study of U.S. Fourth-Grade Mathematics and Science Achievement in International Context.* Washington, D.C.: U.S. Government Printing Office.

U.S. Department of Education. 1997c. "Eighth-Grade Mathematics Lessons: United States, Japan, and Germany." Videotape. Washington, D.C.: U.S. Department of Education.

U.S. Department of Education. 1998. *Pursuing Excellence: A Study of U.S. Twelfth-Grade Mathematics and Science Achievement in International Context.* Washington, D.C.: U.S. Government Printing Office.